# IT'S NEVER JUST AN ACCIDENT

BEYOND THE ACCIDENT: UNDERSTANDING TRAUMATIC BRAIN INJURY AND REBUILDING LIVES

MICHAEL HACKARD, ESQ.

HACKARD GLOBAL MEDIA

Copyright © 2024 by Michael Hackard, Esq.

All rights reserved.

No part of this book may be reproduced in any form or by any electronic or mechanical means, including information storage and retrieval systems, without written permission from the author, except for the use of brief quotations in a book review.

All materials, stories, law, and conclusions contained in this book are for general information only. The information in this book is not legal advice, should not be relied upon as legal advice, may not be current, and is subject to change without notice.

Publisher's Cataloging-In-Publication Data

Names: Hackard, Michael, author.

Title: It's never just an accident : beyond the accident: understanding traumatic brain injury and rebuilding lives / Michael Hackard, Esq.

Description: [First edition]. | [Mather, California] : Hackard Global Media, [2024] | Includes bibliographical references.

Identifiers: ISBN: 978-0-9991446-6-4 (paperback) | 978-0-9991446-7-1 (ebook) | LCCN: 2024911756

Subjects: LCSH: Brain--Wounds and injuries. | Brain damage. | Head--Wounds and injuries. | Brain damage--Diagnosis. | Brain--Wounds and injuries--Complications. | Cognition disorders-- Diagnosis. | Post-concussion syndrome. | Brain--Wounds and injuries--Patients-- Rehabilitation. | Brain damage--Patients--Rehabilitation. | Brain damage--Psychological aspects. | Brain damage--Patients--Services for--United States. | Brain--Wounds and injuries--Law and legislation--United States. | Compensation (Law)--United States. | Brain--Wounds and injuries--United States--Trial practice. | Accident law--United States--Trial practice. | Personal injuries--United States--Trial practice. | BISAC: LAW / Health. | LAW / Disability. | HEALTH & FITNESS / Diseases & Conditions / Nervous System (incl. Brain)

Classification: LCC: RC387.5 .H33 2024 | DDC: 617.4/81044—dc23

Hackard Global Media, LLC

10630 Mather Blvd.

Mather, CA 95655-4125

Printed in the United States of America

*When I first tried to write this dedication, I wanted to simply say, "To my wife, Lisa." But I soon realized that those words cannot capture the depth of my love and gratitude to her.*

*This book is about traumatic brain injury. It helps that I've endured this myself. Family members of traumatic brain injury patients become heroes. In my case it was Lisa who was the one who stood by my side, supporting me and our family every step of the way, even when I could not see or hear the challenges we faced. She was the one who shouldered the burdens, made the plans, and kept our family afloat during the darkest moments.*

*This book, and my life itself, is dedicated to Lisa. She is the foundation upon which my life is built.*

# CONTENTS

1. Unseen Harm: Navigating Life After A Traumatic Brain Injury — 1
2. Recognizing The Signs And Symptoms Of Tbi — 7
3. Navigating the Medical System After a TBI — 17
4. Understanding the Long-Term Effects of a TBI — 24
5. Seeking Legal Guidance and Support — 35
6. Building A Strong TBI Case — 44
7. The Legal Process: What to Expect — 58
8. Securing Compensation and Benefits — 72
9. The Role of Family and Caregivers In TBI Recovery — 84
10. Managing the Financial Implications of TBI — 95
11. Life After TBI: Stories of Hope and Resilience — 107
12. Finding Hope, Empowerment, and Resources After TBI — 121
13. Epilogue: Take the Next Steps — 129
14. A Few Important TBI Medical Resources in California — 137
15. Glossary of Terms — 143

*About the Author* — 161
*Also by Michael Hackard, Esq.* — 163

# 1

# UNSEEN HARM: NAVIGATING LIFE AFTER A TRAUMATIC BRAIN INJURY

**What Are Your Pillars of Strength?**

What are your pillars of strength? Identify them, and in times of crisis, you'll know what sustains you, and you'll be grateful. For anyone who has suffered a traumatic brain injury (TBI), this holds especially true. My faith, family, and friends have helped carry me through life's challenges. And these support systems are critical for anyone who has experienced TBI.

TBI is often called the "silent epidemic." It leaves no visible scars, making it difficult for victims, their loved ones, and even medical professionals to fully grasp the extent of the injury. TBIs can range from mild (mTBI), commonly known as concussions, to severe, with varying symptoms and long-term effects. When a person suffers a brain injury, it is challenging to determine the specific abilities they have lost due to the lack of comprehensive baseline data that would have documented their capabilities prior to the injury.

As C.S. Lewis wisely wrote in *A Grief Observed*, "It is different when the thing happens to oneself, not to others, and in reality, not imagination." Individuals with mild TBI (mTBI) are the walking wounded, appearing unscathed on the surface but grappling with a profound internal battle.

## Recognizing the Symptoms of MTBI & Navigating My Unknown

Anxiety, stress, amnesia surrounding the traumatic event, depression, altered consciousness, and impaired learning are just a few of the common aftereffects of mTBI. It's common that patients struggle to connect their symptoms to the traumatic event, leaving them feeling lost and alone. They may not even realize that they think, feel, or act differently than they did before.

The trauma of mTBI hits like a bolt from the blue – it's unexpected and catches us unprepared. In the words of a former U.S. Secretary of Defense, it's an "unknown unknown," a variable we never had to consider. In my experience, mTBIs can leave individuals unaware of the true nature of their condition and the long-term impact it may have on their lives.

I wrote this book to raise awareness of mTBIs and emphasize the importance of timely diagnosis and treatment. My own experiences have shaped its creation. Without them I would lack the same degree of empathy and insight that I can share with readers today. There's a world of difference between living through a traumatic event and simply reading about it.

A little over thirty years ago, I had an undiagnosed benign brain tumor. I had symptoms – to me, baffling symptoms – but neither I nor my doctors connected the dots. The tumor was truly an unknown unknown. My wife, Lisa, exhibiting better sense than I, insisted on further medical tests. A computed tomography (CT) scan revealed a meningioma. It was pressing on the nearby brain tissue, vessels, and nerves. It sounds strange, but I was relieved to finally connect the dots.

Lisa and I were a team. She led our quest to find the best surgeon to deal with this situation. Surgery was successful – followed by six months of recuperation. It was only through my wife's insistence on additional testing that I received the knowledge and treatment I needed. When faced with a life-changing event, don't be afraid to get a second opinion.

It's well established that a person recovering from brain surgery may have symptoms that are similar to those of people who have suffered a serious brain injury. After all, a portion of the skull is removed, the brain exposed, and surgical procedures are performed on the brain. It's little wonder that the effects of the surgery can feel like you've been struck hard over the head. Fatigue also factored in – it felt like I hadn't slept, as if it was always three o'clock in the morning. There were, of course, headaches as well as difficulty concentrating. Still, I certainly felt better at a year post-surgery than I did during the six months of recuperation.

## A Second Challenge: Adverse Drug Reactions

Just over a year later, in 1994, a drug approved by the FDA and prescribed to me caused me two serious adverse reactions: mild aplastic anemia and the beginnings of liver failure. The drug had been prescribed to manage some of the aftereffects of my tumor. Similar to my bafflement prior to my tumor diagnosis, I had no idea why I felt so bad. I did feel bad, though. I started to give away some of my clothes – thinking that my time left on earth was limited.

Lisa, again my protector, put an end to this. We connected the dots when the drug manufacturer sent a letter to 240,000 physicians advising them to consider taking their patients off the medication after ten people using it developed a frequently fatal form of anemia, and two died. I received first-hand experience dealing with medical misdiagnosis and a physician's failure to listen to his patient.

As an attorney who has personally faced these challenges, I am deeply committed to representing individuals who have suffered TBIs due to others' negligence. My experience taught me that physicians may be reluctant to acknowledge the possibility of adverse reactions to prescription drugs, even when those reactions are well-documented. Disclosing medical errors is challenging, and I know firsthand how patients can be left feeling frustrated and ignored when their concerns are not properly addressed. It is crucial for medical professionals to listen to their patients, take their concerns seriously, and conduct thorough assessments and testing to accurately diagnose and treat conditions like TBIs.

**Turning My Personal Experience into Advocacy**

Motivated by my own experiences in 1994, I soon began representing plaintiffs harmed by withdrawn and/or dangerous pharmaceuticals. Having endured similar struggles, I could empathize with their feelings and the consequences of medical professionals failing to properly assess and diagnose a patient's condition. Now, some 30 years later, this same understanding drives me to represent individuals who have suffered TBIs due to others' negligence. These sufferers are also having a hard time connecting all the dots.

I've learned that TBIs can manifest through various physical, cognitive, behavioral, and perceptual indicators, but without proper diagnosis and testing, patients may be left frustrated and without the necessary care and support. Raising awareness about the signs and symptoms of TBIs and the importance of timely and accurate diagnosis is essential to ensure that those affected receive the care they need.

It's crucial to understand the potential long-term consequences of TBIs. Research has shown that individuals with TBIs have an increased risk of developing neurodegenerative diseases such as Alzheimer's or Parkinson's later in life. TBIs can also have a significant impact on mental health, relationships, and overall quality of life. This information underscores the importance of early diagnosis and proper treatment to mitigate these long-term effects.

Moreover, the economic burden of TBIs on individuals, families, and society as a whole is substantial. Direct medical costs, lost productivity, and the cost of long-term care and support services can be overwhelming. Increasing awareness and support for those affected by TBIs is not only a matter of compassion but also a matter of economic necessity.

Fortunately, there have been significant advances in diagnostic tools and treatments for TBIs in recent years. Improved imaging techniques, biomarkers, and personalized rehabilitation approaches are providing new hope for those affected by TBIs. Ongoing research and development in this field are crucial to improving outcomes and quality of life for TBI survivors.

## The Role of Prevention and Support

While my focus as an attorney is on representing individuals who have already suffered TBIs, I believe it's equally important to emphasize the role of prevention. Promoting safety measures in motor vehicles, encouraging the use of protective equipment in sports and the workplace, and supporting educational campaigns to raise awareness about the risks of TBIs can help reduce the incidence of these life-altering injuries.

Furthermore, I want to acknowledge the crucial role played by family members and caregivers in supporting individuals with TBIs. The challenges faced by caregivers are often overlooked and providing them with resources and guidance is essential to creating a comprehensive support system for TBI survivors.

Throughout my journey, I've encountered inspiring stories of resilience and hope from individuals who have successfully navigated the challenges of living with a TBI. These stories serve as a reminder of the importance of resilience, adaptability, and the power of a strong support system in the recovery process. I encourage readers to act if you suspect that you or a loved one has suffered a TBI and seek prompt medical attention.

To those living with a TBI who may be experiencing verbal outbursts, poor judgment, apathy, depression, or anxiety: know that you are not alone. These symptoms can be challenging for both you and your loved ones, underlining the importance of a dependable support system and access to appropriate medical care. If this book can guide even a few of you or your families toward medical diagnosis and treatment, it will have achieved its purpose – to make a positive difference in the lives of those affected by TBI and to ensure that no one has to face this journey alone.

# 2
# RECOGNIZING THE SIGNS AND SYMPTOMS OF TBI

**Tracy Morgan's Traumatic Brain Injury Journey**

To illustrate the real-life impact of a TBI and the importance of getting medical attention, let's take a closer look at the story of comedian Tracy Morgan and his journey to recovery. On June 7, 2014, Morgan's life changed forever when a Walmart tractor-trailer crashed into his limousine on the New Jersey Turnpike. The accident claimed the life of Morgan's friend and fellow comedian, James McNair, and left Morgan with severe injuries, including a traumatic brain injury.

In the aftermath of the crash, Morgan's condition was critical. He suffered a broken leg, broken nose, and broken ribs, but it was his TBI that posed the most significant challenge to his recovery. As his lawyer, Benedict Morelli, told Today, "There was money involved because that's the only thing that we can use to compensate people who are very injured, and you know that Tracy was close to death."[1]

---

1. https://www.today.com/popculture/tracy-morgan-settles-highway-crash-lawsuit-walmart-t23251

Morgan's road to recovery was long and arduous. He underwent extensive physical therapy and rehabilitation to regain his strength and mobility, but the effects of his TBI lingered. In an interview with Today's Matt Lauer nearly a year after the accident, Morgan shared his ongoing challenges: "I have my good days and my bad days when I forget things. Sometimes, I don't feel well, sometimes emotionally I don't feel well. Now it's just onto the business of getting better and healing."[2]

Morgan's experience is not unique. According to the Centers for Disease Control and Prevention (CDC), each year an estimated 1.5 million Americans sustain a TBI. Fifty thousand people die because of their injuries, while 230,000 are hospitalized and survive. The road to recovery for these individuals is often unpredictable, as Dr. Douglas Smith, a professor of neurosurgery and director of the Center for Brain Injury and Repair at the University of Pennsylvania, explained: "Some become vibrant members of society again, and if you met them, you would never know they had had a brain injury. Others face a lifetime of disability."[3]

For Morgan, the journey to reclaim his life and career was marked by determination and resilience. He continued to undergo therapy and rehabilitation, focusing not only on his physical recovery but also on his cognitive and emotional healing. As he told Lauer, "I can't wait to get back. But right now my goal is just to heal and get better 'cause I'm not 100 percent yet. And when I'm there you'll know it. I'll get back to making you laugh."[4]

Morgan's story is a powerful reminder of the life-altering impact of a TBI and the importance of seeking prompt medical attention and comprehensive rehabilitation. It also highlights the

---

2. https://www.nbcnews.com/nightly-news/tearful-tracy-morgan-says-he-wonders-how-he-will-be-n367906
3. https://www.nbcnews.com/health/health-news/tracy-morgans-brain-injury-recovery-can-last-years-experts-say-n367856
4. Ibid.

individual nature of each TBI journey and the uncertainty that can accompany the recovery process.

TBI can strike without warning, leaving individuals and their loved ones grappling with a new reality. The physical, cognitive, and emotional challenges can be overwhelming, but with the proper care, support, and determination, recovery is possible.

Tracy Morgan's journey is a testament to the human spirit's resilience and the power of hope in the face of adversity. His story inspires us to keep fighting, to seek the help we need, and to never give up on ourselves or our loved ones in the wake of a TBI.

**Common Causes of TBI: The Expected and Unexpected Culprits**

I've worked with TBI survivors for many years and have seen the profound impact these injuries can have on every aspect of their lives. From physical symptoms like headaches and dizziness to the cognitive challenges of memory loss and difficulty concentrating, TBI can turn a person's entire world upside down.

Survivors and their loved ones are left to grapple with a new reality after TBI strikes without warning. And while you may feel terribly alone under the weight of your injury, remember you are not – this is a silent epidemic affecting millions of people each year. The Centers for Disease Control and Prevention (CDC) reports that in 2019, there were approximately 2.87 million TBI-related emergency department visits. This includes 223,135 TBI-related hospitalizations and 60,611 TBI-related deaths. That said, many mild TBIs, such as concussions, go unreported or undiagnosed.

As an attorney with a long career in advocating for people who have been physically or financially injured by the carelessness of others, I've also seen firsthand how TBI injuries can occur in the most unexpected ways.

One of the leading causes of TBI is motor vehicle accidents. Whether you're a driver, passenger, or pedestrian, a sudden collision can result in a violent jolt or blow to the head, leading to brain injury. It's a scenario that plays out far too often on our roads, with countless lives forever changed. Even though cars have gotten safer over the past few decades thanks to technological improvements and more stringent regulations, the number of accidents on our roads continues to be staggering. The California Highway Patrol reported 3,606 fatal crashes and 231,230 injury crashes in California in 2019.

There are numerous types of TBI studies, but they're not all exploring the same data. Some just look at those admitted to trauma centers, while others address emergency room visits. Few assess the time between the trauma and the exhibition of symptoms for those who visit an emergency room but are not hospitalized. For those who are hospitalized after an auto accident, a recent study suggests that about 18% suffered a TBI.

But it's not just car accidents that pose a risk. Falls are another major culprit, particularly among older adults and young children. A slip on an icy sidewalk, a tumble down the stairs, or a misstep on an uneven surface can all lead to a TBI. It's a sobering reminder that even the most mundane activities can have serious consequences.

Sports-related injuries are also a significant cause for concern. From football and hockey to soccer and boxing, the risk of TBI looms large for athletes of all ages. The repeated blows to the head sustained in these high-impact sports can lead to concussions and more severe brain injuries with devastating long-term effects.

And then there are the acts of violence, such as assault and domestic abuse, that can result in a TBI. These intentional injuries are particularly heartbreaking, as they often involve the betrayal of trust by someone close to the victim. These incidents' physical and emotional scars can be profound and long-lasting.

Perhaps most insidious are the emotional and behavioral changes that can accompany a TBI. Mood swings, irritability, depression, and anxiety are all common aftereffects, leaving survivors and their families struggling to cope with a "new normal." It's a journey I know all too well, having faced my own battles with the unknown after my brain tumor diagnosis. The feelings of confusion, frustration, and isolation that come with a brain injury are something no one should have to face alone.

It is crucial for all of us to raise awareness about the common causes of TBI and the importance of seeking medical attention after any blow to the head. Whether it's a car accident, a fall, a sports injury, or an act of violence, the sooner you get a TBI diagnosed and treated, the better the chances for your successful recovery.

**The Physical, Cognitive, and Emotional Aftermath of TBI**

Now that we've discussed the common causes of TBI, let's take a closer look at the wide range of symptoms that can affect TBI survivors. First, knowing that no two cases are exactly alike is essential. The effects can vary widely depending on the severity and location of the injury, as well as a person's unique circumstances. However, some common threads run through many TBI cases, weaving a tapestry of physical, cognitive, and emotional challenges.

Let's start with the physical symptoms. Headaches are one of the most frequently reported aftereffects of a TBI. These headaches can range from mild and occasional to severe and chronic, interfering with daily life and making even the simplest tasks a struggle. Dizziness and balance problems are also common, leaving individuals feeling unsteady on their feet and increasing the risk of falls.

Fatigue is another physical symptom that can be particularly debilitating. It's not just a matter of feeling tired; it's an overwhelming exhaustion that can make it difficult to get out of bed in the morning or stay awake throughout the day. This fatigue can be compounded by sleep disturbances, also common after a TBI.

Vision problems, such as blurred or double vision, sensitivity to light, and difficulty tracking moving objects, can also occur. These issues can make it challenging to read, watch television, or even carry out our basic tasks like cooking or driving. TBI can cause hearing problems, such as tinnitus (ringing in the ears) or difficulty processing auditory information. In some cases, TBI can lead to seizures, which can be especially frightening and debilitating for a survivor and for a caretaker. These might occur in the immediate aftermath of the injury or develop months or even years later. For that reason, people with TBI must work closely with their medical team to manage these physical symptoms and prevent further complications.

Regarding cognitive symptoms, memory loss is one of the most well-known effects of a TBI. A survivor may struggle to remember events from before the injury (retrograde amnesia) or have difficulty forming new memories (anterograde amnesia). Memory issues can make it challenging to keep track of appointments, follow conversations, or even recognize the familiar faces of friends, neighbors, or even family members. Difficulty concentrating and processing information is another common cognitive symptom. Individuals with TBI may struggle to focus on tasks, get easily distracted, or take longer to understand and respond to information. These issues can be particularly frustrating in work or school settings, where the ability to process and retain information is crucial.

Executive functioning skills, such as planning, organizing, and problem-solving, can also be impaired after a TBI, making it challenging to manage daily tasks, make decisions, or adapt to new situations. Individuals may struggle with impulsivity or poor judgment, leading to risky or inappropriate behavior.

Communication problems are also common, both in terms of expressing oneself and understanding others. Individuals with TBI may have difficulty finding the right words, following complex conversations, or interpreting nonverbal cues like facial expressions or tone of voice. Misunderstandings and frustration can occur on both sides.

Finally, there are the emotional and behavioral symptoms of a TBI, which can be some of the most challenging for survivors and their loved ones to navigate. Mood swings and irritability are common, with individuals experiencing rapid shifts between feeling happy, sad, angry, or anxious. These mood changes can be intense and unpredictable, straining relationships and daily life. Depression and anxiety after TBI are a real phenomenon. The combination of physical, cognitive, and emotional challenges can take a toll on mental health, leading to feelings of hopelessness, worthlessness, or constant worry. TBI survivors must have access to mental health support and treatment to manage these symptoms – for their sake and that of their families.

Sometimes, depression manifests as apathy and lack of motivation, with individuals losing interest in activities they once enjoyed or struggling to initiate tasks. People around them might mistake their lethargy for laziness or lack of effort, but it's a genuine symptom of brain injury that requires understanding and support.

Impulsivity and poor impulse control can lead to risky or inappropriate behavior, such as making sudden large purchases, engaging in dangerous activities, or saying hurtful things without thinking. This symptom can be particularly challenging for loved ones to understand and manage. Other personality changes are also possible, with some individuals exhibiting traits or behaviors that seem out of character or different from their pre-injury selves.

While these symptoms are common, they are not inevitable. With proper diagnosis, treatment, and support, many TBI survivors can learn to manage their symptoms and lead fulfilling lives. It's a journey that requires time, patience, and a strong support network.

## The Importance of Seeking Medical Attention: Don't Wait, Investigate

Understanding the potential symptoms of a TBI is essential, but recognizing the need to seek prompt medical attention is equally important. When it comes to TBIs, time is of the essence. The sooner you are medically evaluated, the better your chances of receiving an accurate diagnosis, appropriate treatment, and a positive outcome. But all too often, injury victims might brush off the signs and symptoms of a TBI, thinking they'll just "tough it out" or that their symptoms will go away on their own.

I get it. As someone who has faced my own health challenges, I know how easy it is to downplay your symptoms or convince yourself that you're just being a wimp. But when it comes to your brain, there's no such thing as being too cautious.

The truth is that even a seemingly minor bump on the head can lead to a TBI. You don't have to lose consciousness or experience dramatic symptoms like seizures or memory loss to have sustained a brain injury. Many people with TBI report feeling "off" or "not quite right" after an incident, but they don't necessarily connect those feelings to a potential injury.

That's where the danger lies. When TBI goes undiagnosed and untreated, it can lead to a host of complications down the road. The physical, cognitive, and emotional symptoms we discussed can worsen over time, making it harder to recover and regain quality of life.

However, seeking medical attention isn't just about getting a diagnosis and treatment plan. It's also about protecting your legal rights. If your TBI was caused by someone else's negligence, such as a car accident or a workplace injury, you may be entitled to compensation for your medical expenses, lost wages, and other damages.

If you wait too long to seek medical attention or fail to follow through with your recommended treatment plan, it can be harder to prove the extent of your injuries and the impact they've had on your life. Insurance companies and opposing legal teams may use your delay in seeking treatment as evidence that your injuries aren't as severe as you claim.

That's why it's so crucial to listen to your body and your instincts after any kind of head injury. Don't brush it off or try to power through if something doesn't feel right. Seek medical attention right away, even if you're not sure whether you've sustained a TBI. It's that simple – better safe than sorry.

When you do seek medical attention, it's important to provide a thorough and accurate account of your symptoms and the events leading up to your injury. Don't minimize or downplay your experiences, even if you're worried about being seen as weak or complaining. Your medical team needs to have a complete picture of what you're going through to provide the best care.

In addition to seeking immediate medical attention, following through with any recommended treatment plans or follow-up appointments for cognitive rehabilitation, physical therapy, or mental health counseling is imperative. It can be tempting to skip these appointments or stop treatment once you start feeling better, but it's crucial to see the process through to achieve the best possible outcome.

Even people with access to the best medical care don't always get the immediate help they should. In 2012, NASCAR driver Dale Earnhardt, Jr., sustained a mild TBI (mTBI), also known as a concussion, during a crash at Talladega Superspeedway, one of many he has said to have suffered in his long and successful racing career. An mTBI is a type of traumatic brain injury caused by a bump, blow, or jolt to the head that can change the way your brain usually works. While considered "mild" in comparison to more severe TBIs, concussions can still have grave effects and should be promptly evaluated by a medical professional. Even though he felt "a little odd" after the incident, Earnhardt, Jr., waited several days before seeing a doctor. When he finally did, he was diagnosed and had to sit out for two races.

Looking back on the incident, Earnhardt, Jr., has been vocal about seeking medical attention immediately. In a 2016 interview with USA Today, he noted, "With concussions, anxiety is a huge factor and can be a major problem with people trying to recover."[5]

Earnhardt, Jr.'s, experience is a powerful reminder that even the toughest, most resilient among us need to prioritize our health and well-being after a TBI or even an mTBI. It's not a sign of weakness to seek help; it's a sign of strength and self-care.

So, if you or someone you love has experienced a head injury, don't wait. Seek medical attention right away, even if you're not sure whether you've sustained a TBI. Follow through with your recommended treatment plan, and don't hesitate to reach out for legal and emotional support along the way.

Remember, your brain is your most valuable asset. It's worth protecting, nurturing, and fighting for. With the proper care and support, it is possible to recover from a TBI and reclaim your life. But it all starts with taking that first step and seeking the help you need.

---

5. https://www.usatoday.com/story/sports/nascar/2016/12/03/dale-earnhardt-jr-reflects-on-long-concussion-recovery/94881818/

# 3

# NAVIGATING THE MEDICAL SYSTEM AFTER A TBI

**Dr. Joe's Evolving Symptoms**

The case of Dr. Joe, a former physician who suffered a severe TBI in a car accident, illustrates the complex and evolving nature of TBI symptoms and the importance of comprehensive, ongoing care.[1] The accident left Dr. Joe in a prolonged coma for sixty-three days, followed by ninety-eight days of post-traumatic amnesia. As he emerged from this state, he began to exhibit a wide range of perplexing symptoms that would continue to change over the years.

One of the most striking aspects of Dr. Joe's case was the progressive deterioration of his identity. He lost his sense of self and began to confuse his identity with that of other people. This situation led to a variety of unusual behaviors, such as Dr. Joe claiming to be a six-year-old clone when in the presence of another patient with this delusion, or insisting that he was a twenty-nine-year-old art therapist named Zbyszek when interacting with someone by that name.

---

[1]. https://www.ncbi.nlm.nih.gov/pmc/articles/PMC3524703/

Dr. Joe's memory impairments were profound, affecting not only his autobiographical memory but also his short-term memory. He could retain new information for no more than two hours, after which the memory would be completely lost. He became disoriented and confused as he struggled to understand his surroundings and experiences.

Emotionally, Dr. Joe became highly dysregulated and prone to sudden outbursts of anger or crying. He also exhibited signs of "anosognosia," lacking awareness of his deficits, and "confabulation," creating false narratives to fill in the gaps in his memory. His relationships with his family became strained as they struggled to recognize the man they once knew.

Interestingly, despite these profound changes, Dr. Joe retained much of his medical knowledge. He could still recognize and describe complex medical procedures, such as interpreting an ultrasound image, even as he failed to recognize his own family members or accept his own identity as a physician.

Throughout his recovery, Dr. Joe required the care of a multidisciplinary team of specialists, including neurologists, rehabilitation professionals, and neuropsychologists. They worked together to create a comprehensive treatment plan that addressed his complex needs, adapting their approach as his symptoms evolved.

For example, when Dr. Joe began to exhibit signs of "Capgras syndrome," believing that impostors had replaced his family members, his team had to find ways to help him manage these delusions while still maintaining his engagement in therapy. When he developed what is called "Fregoli syndrome," mistaking strangers for familiar people, his family and caretakers had to develop strategies to help him navigate social interactions safely.

Throughout this process, Dr. Joe's family played a crucial role, even as they struggled to cope with the changes in their loved ones. They participated in his care, provided emotional support, and advocated for his needs, even when he could not recognize them as his flesh and blood.

Dr. Joe's case underscores the importance of a holistic, evidence-based approach to TBI care that considers the full spectrum of a patient's physical, cognitive, emotional, and social needs. It also highlights the need for ongoing monitoring and adaptation of treatment plans, as the effects of a TBI can continue to unfold over months and even years.

By sharing stories like Dr. Joe's, I hope to raise awareness of the complex challenges TBI survivors and their families face and emphasize the critical importance of comprehensive, coordinated care in helping these individuals reclaim their lives and identities. With the right support and resources, even the most profound transformations can be navigated, and new paths can be forged.

### The Importance of Accurate Diagnosis and Early Intervention

When you or someone you love has suffered a traumatic brain injury (TBI), navigating the medical system can feel overwhelming. I know what that's like; I've had the same experience. You may face a barrage of unfamiliar terms, complex procedures, and a team of healthcare professionals from various specialties. You'll want to give up because there are too many medical appointments, too much information, and not enough time. I urge you not to give up. Getting an accurate diagnosis and early intervention can help you take control of your recovery journey and ensure you receive the care and support you need to heal.

Getting diagnosed involves a thorough evaluation by medical professionals who specialize in brain injuries, as well as the use of advanced diagnostic tests and imaging techniques. An accurate diagnosis not only helps determine the severity of the injury but also lays the foundation for an effective treatment plan tailored to your specific needs.

Early intervention is equally critical in the TBI recovery process. The sooner you receive appropriate medical care and begin rehabilitation, the better your chances of achieving a normal life again. Prompt treatment can help minimize the risk of long-term complications, such as chronic headaches, memory problems, and mood disorders, while also promoting the brain's natural healing process.

**Types of Medical Professionals Involved in TBI Care**

TBI care often involves a multidisciplinary team of medical professionals who work together to provide comprehensive treatment and support. Some of the key players in this team may include:

- **Emergency medical personnel:** These first responders, such as paramedics and emergency room doctors, are responsible for stabilizing the patient and assessing the initial severity of the injury.
- **Neurologists:** These physicians specialize in diagnosing and treating brain and nervous system disorders. They play a crucial role in evaluating the extent of the TBI and developing an appropriate treatment plan.
- **Neurosurgeons:** In cases of severe TBI, neurosurgeons may perform surgical interventions to minimize brain damage and promote healing.
- **Rehabilitation specialists:** These healthcare professionals, including physical therapists, occupational therapists, and speech-language pathologists, work with TBI patients to help them regain lost skills and adapt to long-term impairments.
- **Neuropsychologists:** These mental health professionals specialize in assessing and treating the cognitive, emotional, and behavioral effects of brain injuries. They can provide valuable support and guidance throughout the recovery process.

Understanding the roles and responsibilities of each healthcare team member can help you navigate the medical system more effectively and ensure that you receive the comprehensive care you need.

**Diagnostic Tests and Imaging Techniques**

Medical professionals rely on a range of diagnostic tests and imaging techniques to accurately diagnose a TBI and assess its severity. We usually encourage our clients to get all these tests, because each is an essential piece in the puzzle of diagnosing and treating TBI.

Tests include:

- **Computerized Tomography (CT) Scans:** These detailed X-rays of the brain can help detect fractures, bleeding, and other structural abnormalities in the immediate aftermath of a TBI.
- **Magnetic Resonance Imaging (MRI):** This advanced imaging technique uses powerful magnets and radio waves to create detailed brain images, allowing doctors to identify more subtle damage that may not be visible on a CT scan.
- **Neuropsychological Assessments:** These tests evaluate a person's cognitive abilities, such as memory, attention, and problem-solving skills, to determine the extent of any brain dysfunction caused by the TBI.
- **Glasgow Coma Scale (GCS):** This widely used tool helps medical professionals assess a patient's level of consciousness and responsiveness following a TBI, providing valuable information about the severity of the injury.

By combining the results of these diagnostic tests and imaging techniques with a thorough clinical evaluation, medical professionals can develop a comprehensive picture of the TBI and create an individualized treatment plan to support the patient's recovery.

## The Importance of Proper, Evidence-Based Treatment and Referrals to Specialists

When it comes to treating TBIs, receiving prompt, evidence-based care and appropriate referrals to specialists is crucial for optimizing recovery and minimizing the risk of long-term complications. Unfortunately, many patients with TBIs do not receive the comprehensive care they need, often due to a lack of awareness about the severity of their injuries.

One of the most critical aspects of TBI care is ensuring that patients receive treatment grounded in the latest scientific evidence. As our understanding of the brain and the mechanism of injury continues to evolve, and it is constantly doing so, so do the recommended strategies for managing TBIs.

For example, research has shown that while rest is an essential component of early TBI management, prolonged rest and isolation can hinder recovery and make symptoms worse. Instead, a gradual return to normal activities, guided by the patient's tolerance and progress, is now recommended. This approach, known as "active rehabilitation," helps to promote the brain's natural healing processes and prevent the development of secondary issues, such as depression and anxiety.

Another key aspect of evidence based TBI care is the involvement of a multidisciplinary team of specialists. Because TBIs can affect multiple aspects of a person's functioning, including physical, cognitive, and emotional well-being, it is essential to address each of these domains in a coordinated way. TBI victims often need a whole team of healthcare professionals, including neurologists, rehabilitation specialists, neuropsychologists, and others, all working together.

Timely referrals to these specialists can significantly impact a patient's recovery trajectory. For instance, a referral to a neuropsychologist can help identify and manage the cognitive and behavioral changes often accompanying TBIs. In contrast, a physical therapist referral can help address any physical limitations or balance issues.

TBIs aren't like broken bones or appendicitis that can be safely addressed and assumed fixed once there's been appropriate medical care. TBI symptoms may come and go. New and unforeseen issues can crop up at any time. Sometimes, patients never return to "normal" but instead deal with an ever-changing set of problems.

# 4

# UNDERSTANDING THE LONG-TERM EFFECTS OF A TBI

**Spalding Gray's Challenges with TBI**

The case of Spalding Gray, a brilliant actor and writer, is a poignant example of how a TBI can lead to profound changes in personality, mental health, and overall functioning.[1]

In June 2001, Spalding was involved in a serious car accident while on vacation in Ireland. He suffered a broken hip and a fracture to his skull and eye socket, which required surgery. While he initially seemed to recover well, even returning to performing just a few months later, a profound shift occurred in his mental state.

Spalding, who had a history of depression, fell into a deep, obsessive, and seemingly intractable despair. He became consumed with feelings of regret and guilt over decisions he had made, such as selling a beloved family home. His ruminations were relentless, and he found himself unable to engage in activities that had once brought him joy and fulfillment, such as reading and writing.

---

1. https://www.newyorker.com/magazine/2015/04/27/the-catastrophe-oliver-sacks

As his condition deteriorated, Spalding sought help from various medical professionals, including neurologists and psychiatrists. He underwent a range of treatments, from medication to electroconvulsive therapy, but nothing seemed to alleviate his suffering. Neuropsychological testing revealed deficits consistent with damage to his right frontal lobe, the area of the brain that had borne the brunt of the impact during the accident.

What makes Spalding's case particularly tragic is that, before his injury, he had been known for his incredible creativity and his ability to transform personal experiences into compelling narratives that resonated with audiences worldwide. After the accident, however, he felt that he had lost this ability and could no longer achieve the same level of insight and mastery in his work.

This loss of identity, coupled with the unrelenting nature of his ruminations and the profound changes in his personality, put an immense strain on Spalding's relationships with his loved ones. His wife and children struggled to recognize the man they once knew, and Spalding felt increasingly disconnected from the world around him.

Tragically, despite the efforts of his family, friends, and medical team, Spalding ultimately succumbed to his despair. In January 2004, he took his own life, leaving behind a legacy of extraordinary artistic achievement and a powerful reminder of the devastating impact that TBI can have on even the most brilliant and resilient of individuals.

As someone who has dedicated my career to advocating for individuals who have suffered financial and physical harm, including traumatic brain injuries in accidents, from the intentional and careless acts of others, I believe that Spalding's story underscores the critical importance of ongoing support, treatment, and understanding for those grappling with the long-term effects of these injuries. It also highlights the need for continued research into effective interventions and therapies to help individuals like Spalding reclaim their sense of self and find renewed purpose and meaning.

## Navigating the Long-Term Impact: Understanding TBI Survivors' Journey

In this chapter, I'll explore TBI survivors' long-term physical, cognitive, and emotional challenges and how they can impact their relationships and overall quality of life. I'll also discuss why TBIs can lead to brain diseases later in life, which has implications for the importance of ongoing support and care.

I've seen firsthand how these injuries can dramatically alter the course of a person's life. Especially when it comes to TBIs, it is crucial to understand that the effects of these injuries can persist for months, years, or even a lifetime.

A broken bone sustained in a car accident can be severe, but after it heals, there are usually no long-term problems. TBIs are different. A TBI suffered in an accident today may lead to a brain disease in ten, twenty, or even thirty years. It is for that reason that my firm works tirelessly to set up long-term financial plans for victims of TBIs and to make sure that whatever compensation we gain for clients will be enough to see them through for many decades to cover these needs.

### Physical, Cognitive, and Emotional Challenges

The physical, cognitive, and emotional effects of a TBI can be wide-ranging and highly variable from person to person. Common long-term physical challenges include chronic headaches, fatigue, dizziness, and balance problems. These symptoms can make it difficult for TBI survivors to return to work, engage in leisure activities, or even perform the basic activities of daily living.

Cognitive challenges are also a hallmark of TBIs and can persist long after the initial injury. These may include problems with memory, attention, concentration, and executive functioning skills like planning and problem-solving. I've worked with countless clients who struggle to remember appointments, follow conversations, or make decisions, even months or years after their injury.

Emotionally, TBI survivors may experience increased irritability, anxiety, depression, and mood swings. These changes can be particularly challenging for the individual and their loved ones, as they can strain relationships and lead to social isolation.

Family members may not always understand that the challenges faced by TBI survivors are not simply a matter of willpower or motivation. They are the direct result of the damage to the brain and require specialized care and support to manage effectively. That's why, when working with TBI clients, my firm always takes a holistic approach, considering not just the legal aspects of the case but also the ongoing medical, emotional, and practical needs of individuals and their families.

**Sensory Symptoms and Impairments**

In addition to physical, cognitive, and emotional challenges, individuals who have suffered a TBI may also experience sensory symptoms and impairments that can persist long after the initial injury.[2] These sensory issues can significantly impact a person's quality of life and ability to engage in daily activities.

- **Vision:** One common sensory symptom following TBI is blurred vision, accompanied by other visual changes, such as double vision (diplopia) due to damage to eye muscles or nerves and increased sensitivity to light (photophobia), making bright environments uncomfortable. Some individuals may also experience visual processing problems, affecting their ability to recognize objects or patterns. Retinal thinning, which can further affect vision, can occur.

---

2. https://www.ninds.nih.gov/health-information/disorders/traumatic-brain-injury-tbi

Blurred vision, difficulty focusing, and trouble tracking moving objects are also among the visual complaints reported by TBI survivors.
- **Hearing:** Tinnitus, or ringing in the ears, is another frequent complaint among TBI survivors. This persistent buzzing or ringing sound can be highly distracting and contribute to difficulty concentrating and sleeping. In some cases, TBI can also lead to hearing loss, either partial or complete, because of damage to the inner ear or auditory pathways.
- **Taste:** Taste changes are not uncommon following a TBI. Some individuals report a persistent bitter taste in their mouth, while others may experience a loss of taste, affecting their ability to enjoy food and drink.
- **Smell:** Similarly, anosmia (loss of smell) or altered smell perception can occur, which can have implications for safety, such as the inability to detect gas leaks or spoiled food.
- **Touch:** Other sensory impairments may include tingling or pain sensations due to nerve damage.

It's important to note that these sensory symptoms and impairments can vary widely from person to person and may not always be immediately apparent following the injury. In some cases, they may develop or worsen over time, underlining the importance of ongoing monitoring and care for TBI survivors.

As an attorney who represents individuals who have suffered a TBI due to the negligence of others, I have seen how these sensory challenges can compound the already significant burden faced by survivors and their families. The impact on daily functioning, independence, and overall well-being cannot be overstated. That is why it is so crucial for TBI survivors to have access to comprehensive medical care and support services that address not only their physical and cognitive needs but also their sensory impairments. Working with specialists such as neuro-optometrists, audiologists, and occupational therapists can provide targeted interventions and strategies to help manage these symptoms.

Also, the presence of sensory impairments can have significant implications for the legal case of a TBI survivor. These challenges must be properly documented and considered when assessing the full impact of the injury on the individual's life and prospects. By understanding the wide-ranging effects of TBI, including sensory symptoms and impairments, attorneys can better advocate for the rights and needs of survivors and ensure that they receive the care, support, and compensation they deserve.

**Impact on Relationships and Quality of Life**

The long-term effects of a TBI can have a ripple effect on every aspect of a person's life, including their relationships with family, friends, and colleagues. Spouses and partners may find themselves taking on new roles as caregivers while also grieving the loss of the relationship they once had. Children may struggle to understand the changes in their parent and may require additional support and guidance.

Friendships and social connections can also suffer, as the TBI survivor may have difficulty engaging in the activities they once enjoyed or may behave in ways that others find confusing or off-putting. Sometimes, the individual may withdraw from social situations altogether, finding it easier to isolate themselves than navigate interpersonal relationship challenges.

The impact on quality of life can be profound, as the TBI survivor may find themselves unable to return to work, engage in hobbies or leisure activities, or participate in family life in the way they once did. This situation can lead to frustration, loss, and despair and exacerbate the emotional challenges already present.

In my experience, it's also essential to involve the TBI survivor themselves in rebuilding their life to the greatest extent possible. Family members may have to adapt activities and expectations to their current abilities while encouraging the TBI victim to push their boundaries and regain as much independence as possible. It may also mean finding new ways to connect and communicate and being patient and understanding when setbacks occur.

My goal is always to help the TBI survivor reclaim as much of their former life and identity as possible while also supporting them in creating a new path forward. It's a complex and ongoing process, but with the proper care, support, and legal advocacy, it is possible to achieve a fulfilling and meaningful life after a TBI.

## Potential for Developing Neurodegenerative Diseases

One of the most concerning long-term effects of TBIs is the increased risk of developing neurodegenerative diseases later in life. Studies have shown that individuals who have experienced a TBI are at higher risk for conditions such as Alzheimer's disease, Parkinson's disease, and chronic traumatic encephalopathy (CTE).

The exact mechanisms behind this increased risk are not yet fully understood, but it is thought that the inflammation and damage caused by the initial injury may set the stage for the development of these conditions years or even decades later. This fact is particularly concerning given that many of these diseases have no cure and can lead to progressive cognitive decline, physical disability, and eventually death.

As an attorney, I've seen the devastating impact these conditions can have on the individual and the entire family. The financial and emotional costs can be staggering, and the knowledge that a long-ago TBI may have triggered the condition only adds to the sense of loss and frustration.

That's why it's so important for TBI survivors to receive ongoing monitoring and care, even if they appear to have fully recovered from their initial injury. Regular check-ins with a neurologist or other specialist can help to identify early signs of neurodegenerative disease and allow for prompt intervention and treatment.

It's also crucial for TBI survivors and their families to be aware of the potential legal implications of these conditions. In some cases, the development of a neurodegenerative disease may be grounds for a new legal claim, separate from the initial TBI case. An experienced TBI attorney can help to navigate these complex issues and ensure that the individual and their family receive the compensation and support they need.

**Current Research Findings on TBI Recovery**

In the past, it was common for TBI patients to be advised to rest in a quiet, darkened room for weeks or even months after their injury. However, studies have now shown that this approach can hinder recovery and lead to prolonged symptoms and secondary issues.

One of the most concerning potential consequences of prolonged rest is the development of depression and anxiety. When individuals are isolated from their normal activities and social connections for an extended period, they risk developing feelings of loneliness, hopelessness, and despair. These emotional challenges can, in turn, exacerbate the physical and cognitive symptoms of the TBI, creating a vicious cycle that can significantly prolong recovery.

In addition to the emotional impact, prolonged inactivity can lead to physical deconditioning, as the body becomes weaker and less resilient. Furthermore, total sensory deprivation can hinder the brain's natural healing processes. As discussed in the next section, the brain partially recovers from injury by forming new neural connections and rerouting signals through undamaged pathways. However, this process requires some stimulation and activity to occur optimally. By completely shutting down all sensory input, prolonged rest can slow down or stall the brain's recovery.

In recent years, there has been a growing body of research on the most effective strategies for promoting recovery after a TBI. Current guidelines recommend a gradual return to activity, starting with simple tasks and building up to more complex ones as the individual's symptoms allow. Such a recovery might include short walks, listening to calm music, or engaging in gentle stretching or physical therapy exercises.

The key to regaining one's life is to find a balance between allowing the brain to heal and preventing the negative effects of prolonged inactivity. TBI victims can't do it alone. To succeed, close collaboration between the individual, the family, and the medical team and a willingness to adapt the plan is needed.

As an attorney, I encourage my clients to actively participate in their recovery and work closely with their medical team to develop a comprehensive rehabilitation plan. This strategy might include working with a physical therapist to regain strength and coordination, a speech therapist to address communication difficulties, or a neuropsychologist to manage cognitive and emotional challenges.

By staying informed about the latest research and best practices in TBI recovery and by advocating for their own needs and goals, TBI survivors can give themselves the best possible chance of a full and meaningful recovery. By working with an experienced TBI attorney, they can ensure that they have the resources and support they need to focus on their healing journey without the added stress and burden of legal concerns.

**How the Brain Recovers from Concussions**

One of the most remarkable things about the human brain is its ability to adapt and rewire itself in response to injury or damage. This process, known as neuroplasticity, is at the heart of how the brain recovers from concussions and other types of TBIs.

When a concussion occurs, the force of the impact can cause microscopic damage to the delicate nerve fibers in the brain, known as axons. This damage disrupts the normal flow of electrical signals between brain cells, leading to various symptoms of a concussion, such as headache, dizziness, confusion, and memory problems.

However, the brain is not simply a static organ that remains damaged forever after an injury. Instead, it can form new neural connections and reroute signals through undamaged pathways, essentially rewiring itself to compensate for the damaged areas.

This process of neuroplasticity is activated almost immediately after a concussion occurs, as the brain begins to search for alternative routes to transmit signals. Over time, with the right kind of stimulation and support, these new pathways can become stronger and more efficient, allowing the brain to return to its normal functioning.

However, it's important to note that this process is not automatic or guaranteed. For the brain to optimally rewire itself, it needs the right kind of input and activity. Rehabilitation is crucial. By engaging in targeted exercises and activities that challenge the brain in specific ways, TBI survivors can help promote the growth of new neural connections and enhance the efficiency of the rewiring process. A rehab program might include cognitive exercises to improve memory and attention, physical therapy to regain balance and coordination, or occupational therapy to relearn everyday skills.

The key is to provide the brain with the right kind of stimulation at the right time while also being careful not to overload it with too much too soon. I encourage my clients to actively participate in rehabilitation and advocate for the services and support they need to optimize their brain's natural healing processes. I might suggest working with a specialized concussion clinic or rehabilitation center or seeking out targeted therapies such as neurofeedback or cognitive remediation.

By combining cutting-edge medical interventions with a

proactive, engaged approach to recovery, TBI survivors can give themselves the best possible chance of making a full and lasting recovery. By working with an experienced TBI attorney, they can ensure that they have the resources and support they need to focus on their healing journey without the added stress and burden of legal and financial concerns.

# 5
# SEEKING LEGAL GUIDANCE AND SUPPORT

**Conor Gormally's Experience and Struggles as a TBI Survivor**

The challenges TBI survivors face in getting accurate information and appropriate treatment is poignantly illustrated by Conor Gormally, a former Carleton College student, whose life was turned upside down after suffering a concussion during a game of pick-up Frisbee.[1]

Gormally's story is a powerful reminder of how a seemingly minor incident can have profound and long-lasting consequences. After his injury, he was forced to take a medical leave after just one week of the fall term. Despite attempting to return to his studies, he struggled with the ongoing effects of his concussion. He had to take another leave in the spring, delaying his education and putting his future on hold.

What makes Gormally's experience particularly affecting is the realization he had during his recovery process. As a non-athlete, he found that most of the concussion education and

---

1. https://www.carleton.edu/news/stories/changing-the-culture-how-carls-are-conquering-concussions/

research available was geared towards varsity athletes, leaving a significant gap in resources for individuals like himself who sustained concussions in other contexts.

Determined to make a difference, Gormally and his mother founded Concussion Alliance, a nonprofit organization that provides reliable, evidence-based information about preventing and treating concussions accessible to everyone. Through their work, they have created a comprehensive collection of resources specifically designed for college students, including the first-ever college-level, non-sport-specific "Return-to-Learn" plan.

Gormally's story is a testament to the resilience and determination of TBI survivors, as well as the critical importance of advocating for oneself and others in the face of inadequate care and support. By turning his struggles into a mission to help others, he has become a powerful voice for change in concussion education and awareness.

Organizations like Concussion Alliance are invaluable in filling these gaps and empowering individuals to take control of their recovery journey. Seek the support of experienced professionals, including attorneys who advocate for TBI survivors, and take advantage of the growing network of resources and communities dedicated to helping individuals like Conor Gormally rebuild their lives with strength, dignity, and hope.

**Determining if You Have a Potential TBI Lawsuit**

Understanding the factors determining whether you have a potential TBI lawsuit can be a complex process, requiring a careful evaluation of the circumstances surrounding your injury and the applicable laws in your jurisdiction.

As an attorney who has represented numerous TBI survivors and their families, I've seen firsthand the devastating impact these injuries can have on every aspect of a person's life. From mounting medical bills and lost wages to the profound emotional and psychological toll, the consequences of a TBI can be far-reaching and long-lasting.

If you or a loved one has suffered a traumatic brain injury (TBI) due to the negligence or wrongdoing of another party, you may be entitled to legal compensation. However, when assessing whether you have a potential TBI lawsuit, you must consider several key factors. First and foremost, it's essential to determine the cause of your injury and whether another party's actions or inactions contributed to it. Such a determination may include many scenarios, such as a car accident caused by a distracted driver, a slip and fall on a poorly maintained property, or a sports-related injury resulting from inadequate safety protocols.

It's also crucial to evaluate the extent of your injuries and their impact on your life. There may be immediate effects, such as medical expenses and lost income, as well as long-term consequences, such as ongoing rehabilitation needs, diminished earning capacity, and reduced quality of life. In my experience, one of the most challenging aspects of TBI cases is proving the full extent of the harm suffered by the survivor. Unlike more visible injuries, such as broken bones or lacerations, the effects of a TBI may not always be immediately apparent to others. Survivors may struggle with a wide range of cognitive, emotional, and behavioral changes that can be difficult to quantify and communicate to those who have not experienced a similar injury.

Because of the many nuances and non-obvious injuries, the role of an experienced TBI attorney becomes invaluable. By working with medical experts, vocational specialists, and other professionals, a skilled lawyer can help build a compelling case that fully captures the scope of your losses and the impact on your life. A knowledgeable attorney can also navigate the complex legal landscape surrounding TBI cases, ensuring that your rights are protected and you receive the full compensation to which you are entitled.

If you suspect you or a loved one may have a potential TBI lawsuit, seeking legal guidance as soon as possible is essential.

The statutes of limitations for personal injury claims vary by state, and delaying action could jeopardize your ability to recover damages. Also, the sooner you involve an attorney, the more effectively they can gather evidence, interview witnesses, and build a strong case on your behalf.

Sorting through these statutes, requirements, and medical opinions can be an immense challenge. As the head attorney at my firm, Hackard Law, I lead a team committed to providing the compassionate, knowledgeable representation survivors and their loved ones deserve. If you have questions about your legal rights and options following a TBI, I encourage you to contact our team for a free, confidential consultation. Together, we can work to ensure that you receive the support, resources, and compensation you need to move forward with your life.

**Common Types of TBI Lawsuits**

Traumatic brain injuries (TBIs) can occur in a wide variety of circumstances, and the legal remedies available to survivors and their families will depend on the specific facts of each case. However, I have encountered several common types of TBI lawsuits in my practice, each with unique challenges and considerations.

- **Car Accidents:** One of the most frequent sources of TBI lawsuits is car accidents. Whether caused by a distracted, intoxicated, or reckless driver, the forces involved in a motor vehicle collision can easily lead to serious head trauma, even if the victim does not initially lose consciousness. In these cases, it is advisable to have an attorney who understands the complex interplay between TBI's medical and legal aspects and can effectively navigate the insurance claims process while also building a strong liability case.

- **Slip and Fall:** Another common type of TBI lawsuit arises from slip and fall accidents, particularly on commercial properties such as retail stores, restaurants, or office buildings. Property owners and managers have a legal duty to maintain safe conditions for visitors. The consequences can be devastating when they fail to address hazards such as wet floors, uneven surfaces, or inadequate lighting. In these cases, an experienced TBI attorney can help investigate the accident's circumstances, gather evidence of negligence, and hold the responsible parties accountable.
- **Sports Injuries:** Sports-related injuries are also a growing area of TBI litigation, particularly as public awareness of the long-term effects of concussions and repetitive head trauma has increased in recent years. From professional athletes to student competitors, those who suffer TBIs because of inadequate safety protocols, defective equipment, or improper training and supervision may have legal recourse against coaches, schools, leagues, or equipment manufacturers.
- **Assault:** In some cases, TBIs may be the result of physical assault or violence, whether in the context of a criminal attack, a domestic dispute, or an altercation with law enforcement. In these situations, survivors may have civil remedies available in addition to any criminal charges that may be pursued, and an experienced TBI attorney can help coordinate with law enforcement and prosecutors while also advocating for the victim's rights in civil court.

## The Role of an Experienced TBI Attorney

Having an experienced attorney can give you a significant advantage in your efforts to recover your life after a TBI. I have seen evidence of this in my own team that has extensive experience representing TBI survivors and their families in various legal contexts. We understand these cases' unique challenges and complexities, and we have always been committed to providing the personalized, aggressive advocacy our clients need to secure the best possible outcomes.

One of the key advantages of working with an experienced TBI attorney is a deep understanding of the medical and scientific issues involved in these cases. TBIs are complex injuries that can manifest in a wide range of physical, cognitive, and emotional symptoms, many of which may not be immediately apparent or easily diagnosed. An attorney well-versed in TBI cases will have a network of medical experts and consultants who can help assess the extent of the injury properly, develop compelling evidence of its impact on the survivor's life, and communicate this information effectively to insurance companies, judges, and juries.

In addition to their medical knowledge, experienced TBI attorneys also can make an accurate analysis of the legal frameworks and strategies that apply to these cases. They can help survivors and their families to navigate the often-confusing maze of insurance claims, legal deadlines, and procedural requirements, ensuring that their rights are protected and that they do not inadvertently waive any important legal remedies.

Perhaps most importantly, a skilled TBI attorney can serve as a powerful advocate and ally for survivors and their families during what is often the most difficult and traumatic period of their lives. They can provide a listening ear, a voice of reason, and a source of strength and support, helping their clients weather the storms of medical treatment, financial hardship, and legal uncertainty.

I take great pride in my role as an advocate and partner for my TBI clients. It's a commitment to representation rooted in decades of hard work and real-world results. My team also understands that each case is unique, and we take the time to get to know our clients personally, to understand their needs and goals, and to develop customized legal strategies that reflect their circumstances. Whether through aggressive negotiation with insurance companies, skillful navigation of the court system, or compassionate counsel and support, our commitment is to help our clients achieve the best possible outcomes and rebuild their lives with dignity and hope.

**Challenges Faced by Concussion Patients in Receiving Proper Care**

One of the most significant challenges faced by individuals who have suffered concussions and other traumatic brain injuries is the lack of understanding and expertise among many primary care providers and emergency room personnel when it comes to diagnosing and treating TBIs. Because the symptoms of concussion (mTBIs) and TBIs can be subtle and varied, and because they may not always show up on standard imaging tests like CT scans or MRIs, these injuries are often missed or misdiagnosed in the early stages. As a result, patients may be sent home with little more than a recommendation to rest and a promise that their symptoms will resolve on their own when, in fact, they may be suffering from a severe and potentially life-altering injury.

Even when a TBI is appropriately diagnosed, patients may struggle to access the specialized care and rehabilitation services they need to optimize their recovery. Many insurance plans limit coverage for cognitive and physical therapy, mental health treatment, and other essential services, leaving survivors and their families to shoulder the burden of paying for care out of pocket. In addition, there is a shortage of qualified TBI specialists in many parts of the country, particularly in rural and underserved areas, making it difficult for patients to access the expertise they need.

Another significant challenge faced by concussion patients is the lack of clear and consistent guidelines for return to work, school, and other activities. While it is now widely recognized that rest is essential in the early stages of recovery, there is still significant debate and uncertainty around when and how patients should begin to resume their normal activities. Conflicting advice can lead to confusion and frustration for survivors and their families, as well as potential struggles with employers, educators, and other stakeholders who may not understand the nature and extent of the injury.

As an experienced TBI attorney, I have seen firsthand the devastating impact that these challenges can have on the lives of survivors and their families. Without proper diagnosis, treatment, and support, individuals with concussions and other TBIs may struggle with prolonged symptoms, disability, and reduced quality of life, as well as significant financial and emotional strain.

Favorably resolving a client's TBI case depends on more than just attorney excellence. It requires working closely with a network of medical experts, rehabilitation specialists, and other professionals to ensure that clients receive the highest quality care and support. When my own firm represents TBI survivors, we take systematic action to hold insurance companies, employers, and other responsible parties accountable for providing the coverage and accommodations our clients need and deserve.

## Marc Almond, Motorcycle TBI Victim

The story of British singer-songwriter Marc Almond is another powerful example of the life-altering impact of traumatic brain injuries and the incredible resilience of those who survive them. In 2004, Almond was involved in a near-fatal motorcycle accident that left him with severe physical and cognitive impairments, including difficulty speaking, memory loss, and an inability to perform the music that had been his life's passion.[2]

Almond's journey to recovery was a long and arduous one, marked by moments of deep despair and thoughts of suicide. The once-celebrated performer found himself unable to sing, struggling with the most basic tasks of daily living, and facing mounting financial pressures. He described the experience as a "black cloud" hanging over his life, a period of profound uncertainty and fear.

Yet, despite his overwhelming challenges, Almond refused to give up. With the support of loved ones and a team of dedicated medical professionals, he slowly began to rebuild his life and reclaim his identity as an artist. Through tireless work with speech therapists and vocal coaches to regain his ability to sing, he gradually returned to the stage, performing intimate shows showcasing his talent and incredible spirit.

Almond's story is ultimately one of hope and perseverance, a testament to the indomitable human spirit and the power of love, support, and determination in the face of unimaginable adversity. As Almond has said, returning to the stage and sharing his music with the world is the only time he truly feels alive and fulfilled.

For the countless individuals and families whose lives have been touched by traumatic brain injuries, Marc Almond's journey is a beacon of light, a reminder that even in the darkest of times, there is reason to keep fighting, to keep believing in the possibility of a brighter future. As an advocate and an ally, I have always been committed to standing alongside them every step of the way and working tirelessly to ensure they have the resources, support, and legal representation they need to make that possibility a reality.

---

2. https://www.theguardian.com/music/2007/jun/08/popandrock4

# 6

# BUILDING A STRONG TBI CASE

**The Cardona Family**

The Cardona family, driving together in their sedan, was hit by a drunk driver in 2011. They were struck head-on by an SUV that crossed over into their lane.[1] Although there were no immediate signs of a head injury, Mr. Cardona's doctors identified cerebellar damage several years later. He suffered headaches, tremors, slurred speech, dizziness, anxiety, depression, as well as facial numbness and difficulty swallowing.

The trial took thirteen days, and a jury deliberated for two days until a total verdict of nearly $21 million was reached for the family. Of that, economic damages in the amount of $6.3 million were awarded to Mr. and Mrs. Cardona, and non-economic damages of $14.6 million were awarded to all three, with the largest sum, $9.5 million, going to Mr. Cardona.

While this may seem like a significant sum, it's important to remember that this family's life was forever changed by the TBI. The jury assumed that Mr. Cardona would require ongoing care

---

1. https://juryverdictalert.com/dui-accident/cardona-v-cortes

and support for the rest of his life. The compensation awarded ensured he had access to the resources he needed to live as fully and independently as possible.

## Complexities and Challenges of Building the Case

When someone suffers a traumatic brain injury (TBI) due to another person's negligence, building a solid legal case to secure compensation is critical. Unlike most other kinds of personal injury cases, the extent of future problems is often unknowable. A cut on your arm usually heals without further complications, whereas a severe brain injury may not even manifest symptoms for years or decades. Sadly, many victims of TBI don't realize how debilitating these injuries can become. By the time they do understand, statutes of limitations have kicked in – and then it's too late.

As an experienced TBI attorney, I understand the complexities and challenges involved in these cases. Success often hinges on gathering compelling evidence, working with experts, and presenting a clear and persuasive argument for damages.

In this chapter, I'll describe the factors of a strong TBI case, from gathering critical medical records and documentation to working with medical experts who can help establish the extent of your injuries. I will also discuss the importance of calculating economic and non-economic damages and how expert witnesses can provide valuable testimony to support your claim. I'll draw on real-world examples and case studies to illustrate the strategies and techniques that have proven effective in securing successful outcomes for TBI survivors and their families.

## Gathering Medical Records and Documentation

One of the most crucial aspects of building a strong TBI case is gathering comprehensive medical records and documentation that establish the nature and extent of your injuries. This evidence forms the foundation of your case and is essential for proving both liability and damages.

As an attorney, one of my priorities is to obtain all relevant medical records related to your TBI, including:

- Ambulance and emergency room records
- Hospital records, including admission and discharge summaries, progress notes, and test results
- Diagnostic imaging reports, such as CT scans, MRIs, and X-rays
- Records from specialists, such as neurologists, neurosurgeons, and rehabilitation physicians
- Therapy records, including physical therapy, occupational therapy, and speech therapy
- Mental health records, including assessments and treatment notes from psychologists or psychiatrists
- Medication lists and pharmacy records

In addition to medical records, my team and I also work to gather other necessary documentation that can help support the case, such as:

- Police reports and accident scene photographs
- Witness statements
- Employment records, including pay stubs and tax returns
- School records, if the TBI has impacted your education or training
- Journal entries or other personal accounts of your symptoms and challenges

Obtaining these records can be time-consuming and complex, often requiring multiple requests and follow-ups with healthcare providers, employers, and other entities. At my law firm, we handle this process, ensuring we have a complete and accurate record of the survivor's injuries and losses.

Once we've gathered all the necessary documentation, we carefully review and organize these records to create a clear and compelling narrative of your case. We use this evidence to establish the severity of your TBI, the impact it has had on your life, and the ongoing challenges and expenses you may face because of your injuries.

The quality and thoroughness of your medical records can significantly impact the strength of your case. Therefore, receiving prompt medical attention after a TBI and following through with all recommended treatment and follow-up care is critical. The more comprehensive and consistent your medical records are, the stronger your case will be.

In addition to gathering existing records, we may also recommend that you undergo additional medical evaluations or assessments to document the extent of your injuries further. For example, we may refer you to a neuropsychologist for cognitive testing or a vocational specialist to assess your ability to return to work.

As we gather and review your medical records and documentation, we'll build a team of experts who can provide valuable testimony to support your case. In the next section, we'll explore how working with medical experts can help establish the extent of your injuries and strengthen your claim for damages.

Building a strong TBI case takes time, effort, and expertise. But with a skilled and dedicated attorney, you can have confidence that your case is in good hands and that you're taking the proper steps to secure the compensation you'll need for long-term recovery.

## Working with Medical Experts to Establish the Extent of the Injury

In a traumatic brain injury (TBI) case, medical experts play an essential role in establishing the extent of your injuries and the impact they have had on your life. These experts offer valuable insight and testimony that can help strengthen the case. When I act as your attorney, one of my key responsibilities is to identify and work with the right medical experts who can effectively communicate the severity of your TBI and its long-term consequences.

When most people think of medical experts in a TBI case, they often focus on the obvious specialties, such as neurology, neurosurgery, and rehabilitation medicine. While these experts are undoubtedly important, many other medical professionals can provide valuable testimony and support for your claim. Some of these less obvious but equally critical experts may include:

- **Neuropsychologists:** These experts assess brain injuries' cognitive, emotional, and behavioral impacts. They can administer detailed tests to evaluate your memory, attention, problem-solving skills, and other mental functions. They also provide testimony on how your TBI has affected your ability to work, learn, and engage in daily activities.
- **Occupational and vocational specialists:** These experts can assess your ability to return to work or school after a TBI and provide testimony on the accommodations or modifications needed to perform your job or continue your education. They can also help calculate the long-term financial impact of your injuries on your earning capacity and career prospects.
- **Life care planners:** Creating comprehensive plans that outline the ongoing medical care, therapy, and

support services you may need throughout your lifetime due to your TBI is the role of life care planners. They can provide detailed cost estimates for these services, which can be crucial in establishing the full extent of your damages.
- **Neuroimaging specialists:** While CT scans and MRIs are commonly used to diagnose TBIs, many other advanced imaging techniques can provide a more detailed picture of the damage to your brain. These may include diffusion tensor imaging (DTI), functional MRI (fMRI), and positron emission tomography (PET) scans. Neuroimaging specialists can interpret these complex scans and provide testimony on the specific areas of your brain affected by your injury.
- **Neuropsychiatrists:** Psychiatric and behavioral changes can occur because of impacts on the brain. Neuropsychiatrists can provide testimony on conditions such as depression, anxiety, personality changes, and impulse control disorders that may result from a TBI. They can also assess your need for ongoing mental health treatment and support.

In addition to these specific types of experts, it's essential to work with medical professionals with experience treating and evaluating TBI patients. These experts should be able to clearly explain complex medical concepts in a way that a judge and jury can understand, and they should be prepared to defend their opinions under cross-examination.

When working with medical experts, we always consider the timing of their evaluations and testimony. Sometimes, waiting until you have reached maximum medical improvement (MMI) may be necessary before conducting certain assessments or obtaining expert opinions. MMI is the point at which your condition has stabilized and is not expected to improve further with additional treatment. By waiting until you have reached MMI, we can ensure we have an accurate picture of your long-term prognosis and care needs.

While medical experts provide us with healthcare, it's important to understand that they are not direct advocates for you or your long-term treatment. When I call medical experts to the witness stand, all I hope to get from them is objective and unbiased opinions based on their professional expertise and evaluation of my client's condition. My job is to use medical testimony and opinions to build the strongest possible case on my client's behalf.

Clients sometimes assume their doctor is "in their corner" and "has their back." Unfortunately, that's not how the system works. Doctors and healthcare providers may care deeply about you and may work extremely hard to help you recover, but they will not proactively help you to receive compensation for your injuries. Remember, your lawyer is your only advocate and the only one who will fight for you.

**Expert Witnesses in Your Corner**

In addition to medical experts who can provide testimony about the extent of your traumatic brain injury (TBI), other types of expert witnesses can play a crucial role in building a strong case and attaining the compensation you need. These experts can help establish liability, calculate damages, and provide compelling testimony that can sway a judge or jury in your favor.

Some of the key types of expert witnesses who may be involved in a TBI case include:

- **Accident reconstruction experts:** To help jury members visualize what happened, accident reconstruction experts use forensic analysis, computer simulations, and other techniques to recreate the circumstances of the accident that caused your TBI.

They can testify to factors such as speed, impact forces, and the positions of vehicles or objects involved in the crash. This information can establish liability and demonstrate how the other party's negligence caused your injuries.

- **Vocational rehabilitation experts:** How do you know if you can return to work after a TBI? A vocational rehabilitation expert can assess your abilities. Their testimony will address the impact your injury has had on your earning capacity. They can evaluate your skills, experience, and limitations and provide opinions on the types of jobs you can perform and the accommodations you may need. This information can be important in calculating your lost wages and future earning potential.
- **Life care planning experts:** As mentioned earlier, life care planners create comprehensive reports detailing the ongoing medical care, therapy, and support services you may need throughout your lifetime. They can testify to the cost of these services and their impact on your quality of life.
- **Economics experts:** To calculate your lost wages, future earning potential, and the value of your non-economic damages, economics experts are called in. They can use statistical analysis and other methods to calculate the present value of your future losses and provide opinions on the overall economic impact of your injury.
- **Neuropsychology experts:** When it comes to testimony on the cognitive, emotional, and behavioral impacts of your TBI, neuropsychology experts are usually needed. They can explain how your injury has affected your memory, attention, decision-making, and other mental functions and how these impairments may impact your ability to work, learn,

and engage in daily activities. Their information can be important in establishing the full extent of your non-economic damages.

When selecting expert witnesses for your TBI case, working with professionals with extensive experience in their field and a track record of providing clear, persuasive testimony is essential. Your attorney should carefully vet potential experts and ensure their opinions are based on sound scientific principles and methodologies.

I also think it's important to consider how a judge or jury will perceive your expert witnesses. In some cases, it may be helpful to have experts who can relate complex medical or technical concepts in a way that is easy for laypeople to understand. An experienced attorney should work with experts to prepare them for trial and anticipate potential challenges or counterarguments from the opposing side.

## Calculating Economic and Non-Economic Damages

When you've suffered a traumatic brain injury (TBI) due to someone else's negligence, damages can be both economic, which have a clear financial value, and non-economic, which are more subjective and difficult to quantify. It's the TBI attorney's job to work with experts and gather evidence to calculate the full extent of your losses and ensure that you're fairly compensated for how your injury has impacted your life.

### *Economic Damages*

Economic damages are the tangible financial losses you've experienced because of your TBI. These may include:

- **Medical expenses:** This includes all the costs associated with your initial treatment, hospitalization, surgery, medication, and ongoing rehabilitation and therapy. For example, if you require a craniotomy to relieve pressure on your brain, the surgical fees, hospital stay, and follow-up care could easily exceed $100,000.

- **Lost wages:** If your TBI has prevented you from working temporarily or permanently, you may be entitled to compensation for your lost income. The amount of lost wages can be calculated based on your previous earnings history and projections of your future earning potential. For instance, if you earned $50,000 per year before your injury and were expected to miss two years of work, your lost wages would be valued at $100,000.
- **Future medical costs:** Depending on the severity of your TBI, you may require ongoing medical care and support for years or even decades after your initial injury. These costs can be estimated with the help of medical experts and life care planners. For example, if you require daily in-home care and regular therapy sessions, the lifetime cost of these services could exceed $1 million.
- **Property damage:** If your TBI was caused by a car accident, you may also be entitled to compensation for the damage to your vehicle and any other personal property that was lost or damaged in the crash.
- To calculate your economic damages, attorneys work with experts to gather documentation of your expenses, such as medical bills, pay stubs, and repair estimates. They may also consult with economists and financial planners to project your future losses and care needs.

*Non-Economic Damages*

Non-economic damages are the intangible losses you've

suffered because of your TBI, which don't have a clear financial value but can still have a significant impact on your life. These may include:

- **Pain and suffering**: Pain and suffering is a term you'll hear a lot in the law. It often includes the physical pain, discomfort, and emotional distress you've experienced because of your injury. For example, suppose you suffer from chronic headaches, memory loss, and depression after your TBI. In that case, you may be entitled to compensation for the impact these symptoms have on your quality of life.
- **Loss of enjoyment of life**: If your TBI has prevented you from engaging in activities you once enjoyed, such as hobbies, sports, or social events, you may be compensated for this loss. For instance, if you were an avid hiker before your injury but can no longer walk without assistance, this would be a significant loss of enjoyment.
- **Loss of consortium**: This refers to the impact your TBI has had on your relationship with your spouse or partner, including the loss of companionship, affection, and intimate relations. For example, if your personality changes and mood swings have caused a strain in your marriage, this could be considered a loss of consortium.

Calculating non-economic damages can be more challenging, as there is no precise formula or guidelines for assigning a monetary value to these losses. In some cases, attorneys may use a multiplier method, where they multiply the total economic damages by a factor (usually between 1.5 and 5) to arrive at a figure for non-economic damages. For example, if your economic damages are $500,000 and a multiplier of 3 is used, your non-economic damages would be valued at $1.5 million.

Another approach is the per diem method, where a daily rate is assigned for your pain and suffering, and this rate is multiplied by the number of days you've experienced symptoms. For instance, if a daily rate of $200 is used and you've experienced symptoms for 500 days, your non-economic damages would be valued at $100,000. Ultimately, the value of your non-economic damages will depend on the specific facts of your case, the severity of your injuries, and the persuasiveness of your attorney's arguments.

**Tracy Morgan's TBI Lawsuit**

In the case of comedian Tracy Morgan, whose case we considered in Chapter Two, expert witnesses played a key role in securing a significant settlement for Morgan and his fellow passengers. Morgan suffered a severe TBI in a car crash involving a Walmart truck.

Some pieces of evidence and expert testimony presented in the case included:

- Accident reconstruction analysis showed that the Walmart truck driver had been awake for over 28 hours during the crash and had failed to slow down despite posted warning signs.
- Medical records and testimony from neurologists and other experts detailed the extent of Morgan's brain injury, which left him in a coma for two weeks and required months of intensive rehabilitation.
- A vocational and economic analysis demonstrating the impact Morgan's TBI had on his ability to work and earn a living as a comedian and actor.
- Life care planning testimony outlining the ongoing medical care and support services Morgan would need because of his TBI.

While the exact terms of the settlement were not disclosed, it was reported to be a substantial sum that would provide for Morgan's ongoing care and compensate him for his lost earnings and non-economic damages.

**Other Real-World TBI Lawsuits and Evidence**

Though detailed information about the specific evidence used in other TBI lawsuits is generally unavailable, several notable cases illustrate the types of claims and strategies that may be involved:

The case of Drew Bianchi, a pre-med student at UC Davis who was a passenger in a car hit by two big rig trucks that collided head-on in 2007.[2] One truck driver had had only 3 hours of sleep the night before the accident, and the other was talking on his cell phone at the time of impact. Bianchi was awarded $3.4 million for medical expenses, $27.5 million for future medical expenses, $4.5 million for lost wages, and $13.5 million in general damages – a total of $49.1 million.

The case of a South Carolina young college woman whose car was broadsided by a 90,000-pound cement truck going forty-five miles an hour.[3] The driver was both inexperienced and sleep-deprived. The accident victim was able to finish her college degree in accounting but could not pass the CPA exam, which made her essentially unemployable. She eventually received a $3 million settlement.

The case of Thomas East, a thirty-seven-year-old customer service rep who was driving his pickup truck on Christmas Eve 2014 when he was hit by a tractor-trailer, causing his pickup to flip to its roof.[4] Investigators found that the truck driver was

---

2. https://www.lawyersandsettlements.com/legal-news/brain_injury/lawyer-randall-scarlett-12874.html
3. https://www.lawyersandsettlements.com/legal-news/brain_injury/interview-brain-injury-traumatic-14680.html
4. https://www.lawyersandsettlements.com/legal-news/personal-injury/texas-brain-injury-plaintiff-award-20963.html

distracted and had argued with his wife in five separate calls fifteen minutes before the collision. The parties settled for $3.35 million as the case was headed for trial.

These cases demonstrate the wide range of circumstances that can lead to a TBI and the types of parties that may be held liable. They also illustrate the importance of expert testimony in establishing the extent of the plaintiff's injuries and the long-term impacts on their life and livelihood.

In each case, the plaintiffs worked with skilled attorneys and a team of experts to build a strong case and secure the compensation they needed to rebuild their lives. This is always my goal as a TBI attorney. By presenting compelling evidence and expert testimony, they demonstrated the defendants' negligence and the profound impact their injuries had on every aspect of their lives to achieve the best possible outcomes for the clients and their families.

# 7

# THE LEGAL PROCESS: WHAT TO EXPECT

**The Legal Resolution of Tracy Morgan's TBI Lawsuit**

On June 7, 2014, comedian Tracy Morgan was severely injured in a crash on the New Jersey Turnpike when a Walmart truck rear-ended the limousine he was traveling in. The accident killed Morgan's friend and fellow comedian, James McNair, and left Morgan with a traumatic brain injury (TBI), broken leg, and broken ribs. The crash and its aftermath provide a compelling example of the legal process in a high-profile TBI case.

Shortly after he entered the hospital, Morgan retained a law firm. Morgan's attorneys filed a lawsuit against Walmart, alleging that the company should have known that its driver, Kevin Roper, was fatigued and that the company was negligent in its oversight of its drivers. The lawsuit sought punitive and compensatory damages for Morgan and the other passengers in the limousine.

Walmart initially responded to the lawsuit by filing court documents claiming that Morgan and his travel companions were partly to blame for their injuries because they were not wearing seat belts at the time of the crash. This "blame-shifting" tactic is not uncommon in personal injury cases, as defendants may try to find ways to reduce their liability.

However, Morgan and his attorneys quickly fired back, with Morgan releasing a statement saying, "I can't believe Walmart is blaming me for an accident that they caused. My friends and I were doing nothing wrong." His attorneys added, "Tracy Morgan is struggling to recover, and they answer and blame him and the other victims for what they caused. That's despicable."

As the case progressed, Morgan's attorneys used a variety of legal strategies to build a strong case and put pressure on Walmart to settle. They gathered evidence about Roper's lack of sleep before the crash and Walmart's alleged negligence in overseeing its drivers. They also worked with medical experts to document the extent of Morgan's injuries and the long-term impact they would have on his life and career.

In court filings, Morgan's attorneys painted a stark picture of his struggles to recover, with his lawyer Benedict Morelli stating, "He's fighting to get better, and if there's a chance for him to be back to the Tracy Morgan he once was, he's going to try to do that. But we just don't know because of the severity of the injuries that he sustained and the fact that he had such a severe brain injury."[1]

Eventually, the combination of solid evidence, compelling victim testimony, and public pressure led Walmart to settle the case out of court in May 2015, nearly a year after the crash. The settlement terms were confidential, but Morelli expressed satisfaction with the outcome. Morgan released a statement saying, "Walmart did right by me and my family, and for my associates and their families. I am grateful that the case was resolved amicably."[2]

The comedian acknowledged the profound impact the crash and his injuries had on him, but he also expressed a desire to

---

1. https://www.nytimes.com/2014/11/19/nyregion/tracy-morgan-fighting-to-recover-from-severe-brain-injury-lawyer-says.html
2. https://www.npr.org/sections/thetwo-way/2015/05/27/410123505/tracy-morgan-wal-mart-settle-lawsuit-over-truck-limousine-crash

move on with his life and career. Speaking for his client, Morelli noted, "He has a new lease on life."

## What to Expect

The Tracy Morgan case illustrates the complex legal and emotional journey that many TBI survivors face in the aftermath of a devastating crash. The case also highlights the importance of having a skilled and tenacious legal team to advocate for the rights of TBI victims and hold negligent parties accountable.

Let's walk through the usual stages of a TBI lawsuit, from the initial consultation and investigation to filing a complaint, the discovery process, and the potential for mediation, settlement, or trial. You may be worried about how much it will cost to hire an attorney, so I'll talk about the option of choosing contingency fees over hourly rates. I'll also discuss the unique aspects of TBI cases and how they may impact the legal strategy and timeline. By the end of this chapter, you'll have a clear understanding of what to expect when you work with an experienced TBI attorney and how a firm like Hackard Law can help you secure the compensation and support you need to move forward with your life.

### *The Initial Consultation and Investigation*

The legal process begins when you enter our office for your initial consultation. During this meeting, we sit down with you to discuss the details of your case, including how your TBI occurred, the extent of your injuries, and the impact the incident has had on your life and your family. We also ask about any medical treatment you've received, any communication you've had with insurance companies or other parties involved in the incident, and any documentation or evidence you may have collected.

At this stage, our primary goal is to gather as much information as possible to determine the strength of your case and the potential for pursuing a legal claim. We ask questions to help us understand the full scope of your damages, including your medical expenses, lost wages, and the physical, emotional, and psychological impacts of your injury.

Once we've gathered the initial information about your case, we conduct a thorough investigation to identify all potential liability and insurance coverage sources. This step may involve reviewing police reports, medical records, and other documentation related to the incident, as well as interviewing witnesses and consulting with experts in fields such as accident reconstruction, medicine, and vocational rehabilitation.

Based on the results of our investigation, we provide you with an honest assessment of your case and our recommendations for moving forward. If you have a strong claim, we work with you to develop a comprehensive legal strategy tailored to your unique needs and goals.

### *Understanding Contingency Fees in TBI Cases*

When considering hiring an attorney to represent you in a TBI lawsuit, one of the most important factors is how legal fees will be handled. In most TBI cases, attorneys work on a contingency fee basis, meaning they only receive payment if they successfully recover compensation on your behalf.

Contingency fees allow individuals and families affected by TBI to access high-quality legal representation without paying substantial costs upfront. However, it's necessary to clearly understand how contingency fees work and what you can expect when you enter into this type of agreement with an attorney.

### *How Contingency Fees Work*

Under a contingency fee arrangement, your attorney agrees to represent you in your TBI case without charging any upfront fees. Instead, they will receive a percentage of any settlement or jury award they secure on your behalf. The specific percentage can vary depending on the complexity of the case and the stage at which it is resolved, but it is typically in the range of 33% to 40%.

For example, suppose your attorney negotiates a settlement of $1 million on your behalf, and their contingency fee is 35%. In that case, they will receive $350,000 as their fee, and you will receive the remaining $650,000 (before any applicable expenses or liens are deducted). Suppose your case goes to trial, resulting in a jury award of $2 million, and your attorney's contingency fee is 40%. In that case, they will receive $800,000 as their fee, and you would receive the remaining $1.2 million (again before any applicable expenses or liens are deducted).

In addition to the contingency fee, clients may be responsible for certain expenses related to their case, such as court filing fees, expert witness fees, and obtaining medical records and other documentation. These expenses are typically deducted from the client's portion of the settlement or award, not the attorney's fee.

*Advantages of Contingency Fees*

There are several key advantages to working with an attorney on a contingency fee basis in a TBI case:

- **No upfront costs:** You don't have to pay any legal fees out of pocket, which can be a significant relief if you're already facing mounting medical bills and other expenses related to your injury.
- **Alignment of interests:** Because your attorney only gets paid if they secure compensation on your behalf, their interests are aligned with yours in pursuing the best possible outcome for your case.
- **Access to high-quality representation:** Contingency fees allow you to hire an experienced and skilled TBI attorney who may otherwise be out of your price range if you had to pay hourly fees.

- **Motivation to maximize your recovery:** Since your attorney's fee is a percentage of your overall recovery, they have a strong incentive to work hard to maximize your compensation.

*Disadvantages of Contingency Fees*

While contingency fees offer many benefits for TBI plaintiffs, there are also some potential drawbacks to consider:

- **Higher overall fees:** Because attorneys take on significant risk by working on a contingency basis, their fees may be higher than if they were charging hourly rates.
- **Less control over the case:** Since your attorney has a financial stake in the outcome of your case, they may be more likely to push for a settlement rather than taking the case to trial, even if you prefer to have your day in court. Remember that going to trial often carries considerable risk and expense, and there is never a guaranteed 100% win. Whether or not to pursue a trial is a decision that must be carefully weighed by both you and your attorney.

*Choosing the Right TBI Attorney*

When you're considering hiring a TBI attorney on a contingency fee basis, choosing someone with the experience, skill, and integrity to represent your interests effectively is essential. Some key factors to consider include:

- **Track record of success:** Look for an attorney with a proven track record of securing significant settlements and jury awards in TBI cases like yours.
- **Clear communication:** Your attorney should be able to clearly explain their contingency fee structure and

any other costs or expenses you may be responsible for.
- **Compassion and dedication:** Choose an attorney who demonstrates genuine compassion for your situation and a commitment to fighting for the compensation and support you deserve.
- **Resources and expertise:** Make sure your attorney has access to the medical experts, investigators, and other resources necessary to build a strong case on your behalf.

Experienced and reputable TBI attorneys should be open and transparent in answering any questions about contingency fee structures or any other aspect of the legal process in a TBI case. Ensure that you are seeking out high-quality and compassionate representation.

### *Filing a Complaint and Initiating Legal Action*

In our process at Hackard Law, if we determine that pursuing a legal claim is in your best interests, the next step is to file a complaint with the appropriate court. In a TBI case, the complaint will typically name one or more defendants who we believe are legally responsible for your injuries, such as a negligent driver, a property owner, or a product manufacturer. In a lawsuit, the party or parties filing a suit is always called the plaintiff(s), and the party or parties being sued are the defendant(s).

The complaint will outline the specific allegations against each defendant, the legal basis for your claim (such as negligence or strict liability), and the damages you seek. In a TBI case, these damages may include:

- Medical expenses, both past and future
- Lost wages and earning capacity
- Pain and suffering

- Emotional distress
- Loss of enjoyment of life
- Punitive damages (in cases of particularly egregious conduct)

Once the complaint is filed, the defendants can respond, typically by filing an answer denying the allegations or asserting various legal defenses. In some cases, the defendants may also file a counterclaim against you or bring in additional parties they believe are responsible for your injuries.

Understand that filing a complaint does not necessarily mean your case will go to trial. Most TBI cases are resolved through settlement negotiations or alternative dispute resolution processes such as mediation or arbitration. However, filing a complaint is essential in preserving your legal rights and putting pressure on the defendants to take your claim seriously.

### *The Discovery Process and Depositions*

After the complaint is filed and the defendants have responded, the next stage of the legal process is known as discovery. During this phase, both sides can exchange information and evidence related to the case, including documents, photographs, and expert reports.

The deposition process is one of the most important aspects of discovery in a TBI case. A deposition is a formal, out-of-court testimony given under oath and recorded by a court reporter. In a TBI case, depositions may be taken of various parties and witnesses, including:

- The plaintiff (you)
- The defendants
- Eyewitnesses to the incident
- Medical professionals who treated your injuries
- Expert witnesses retained by either side

During a deposition, attorneys for both sides can ask questions and elicit testimony about the incident, your injuries, and other relevant issues. As the plaintiff, you can expect to be asked about your background, your recollection of the incident, your medical treatment, and the impact your injuries have had on your life. You must be well-prepared for your deposition and work closely with your attorney to understand the types of questions you may be asked and how to respond effectively. Your attorney will also be present during the deposition to object to improper questions and protect your legal rights.

In addition to depositions, the discovery process may involve other methods of gathering information, such as interrogatories (written questions that must be answered under oath), requests to produce documents, and requests for admission (asking the other side to admit or deny specific facts).

The discovery process can be lengthy and complex, particularly in cases involving severe TBI and multiple defendants. However, discovery is an essential step in building a strong case and preparing for the possibility of trial.

### *Mediation, Settlement, and Preparing for Trial*

As the discovery process unfolds and both sides gain a clearer picture of the strengths and weaknesses of the case, there may be opportunities for resolution through mediation or settlement negotiations.

Mediation is a form of alternative dispute resolution in which a neutral third party (the mediator) works with both sides to reach a mutually acceptable settlement. In a TBI case, mediation can sometimes effectively avoid a trial's time, expense, and uncertainty while still achieving a fair outcome for the plaintiff. During mediation, the mediator will typically meet with both sides separately to discuss their positions and explore potential areas of compromise. The mediator may also convey settlement offers and counteroffers between the parties and objectively assess the strengths and weaknesses of the case.

If mediation is successful, the parties will sign a settlement agreement outlining the terms of the resolution, including the amount of compensation to be paid and any other conditions or requirements. If mediation is unsuccessful, the case will proceed to trial.

Even if mediation does not result in a settlement, the process can still be valuable in clarifying the issues in dispute and narrowing the focus of the case as it moves forward. Your attorney will use the information gathered during mediation to refine their trial strategy and prepare for the possibility of presenting your case to a judge and jury.

Preparing for trial in a TBI case involves significant work and coordination among your legal team, medical experts, and other key witnesses. Your attorney will work closely with you to develop a compelling narrative of your case, from the circumstances of the incident to the full extent of your injuries and the impact on your life and your family.

As the trial date approaches, your attorney will also engage in intensive preparation with expert witnesses, such as medical professionals and life care planners, to ensure that their testimony is clear, persuasive, and can withstand cross-examination by the defense.

Throughout the trial process, your attorney should be your strongest advocate, workingto present the most compelling case possible on your behalf. While the outcome of any trial is inherently uncertain, with the right legal team, you can rest assured they will be fully committed to achieving the best possible result for you and your family.

The goal of any TBI lawsuit is to secure the compensation and support you need to move forward with your life and adapt to the challenges of your injury. By working closely with an experienced TBI attorney and understanding the stages of the legal process, you can confidently approach your case and focus on what matters most: your health, well-being, and future.

## Understanding the Timeline and Costs of a TBI Lawsuit

When considering whether to pursue a TBI lawsuit, it's natural to have questions and concerns about how long the process will take and how much it will cost. While every case is unique, and there is no one-size-fits-all answer to these questions, some general guidelines and considerations can help you understand what to expect.

*Timeline of a TBI Lawsuit*

The timeline of a TBI lawsuit can vary significantly depending on factors such as the complexity of the case, the number of parties involved, and whether the case settles or goes to trial. However, here is a general overview of the stages of a TBI lawsuit and the estimated time each stage may take:

Initial consultation and investigation: 1-3 months

- Meeting with an attorney to discuss your case
- The attorney conducts a preliminary investigation and gathers evidence
- The attorney assesses the strengths and weaknesses of your case
- Filing a complaint and serving the defendant(s): 1-3 months
- The attorney drafts and files a complaint with the court
- Defendant(s) are served with the complaint and summons
- Defendant(s) file an answer or other response

**Discovery: 6-12 months**

- Parties exchange information and evidence
- Depositions are taken of witnesses and experts
- Parties may file motions to compel or limit discovery
- Mediation or settlement negotiations: 1-3 months
- Parties may attempt to resolve the case through mediation or informal negotiations
- If a settlement is reached, the case concludes

**Trial preparation: 2-4 months**

- If the case does not settle, attorneys prepare for trial
- Expert witnesses are prepared for testimony
- Exhibits and demonstrative aids are finalized

**Trial: 1-3 weeks**

- The case is presented to a judge or jury
- Witnesses and experts testify
- Judge or jury renders a verdict

**Post-trial motions and appeals: 6-12 months or longer**

- Parties may file motions for a new trial or to modify the judgment
- Parties may appeal the verdict to a higher court

As you can see, the entire process, from initial consultation to final resolution, can take several months to several years. However, remember that most TBI cases are resolved through settlement, which can significantly shorten the timeline.

*Costs of a TBI Lawsuit*

As discussed in the previous section on contingency fees, most TBI attorneys work on a contingency fee basis, meaning you do not pay any upfront costs for legal representation. However, there are still some costs associated with pursuing a TBI lawsuit that you should be aware of:

- **Case expenses:** These are costs related to the investigation and preparation of your case, such as fees for obtaining medical records, hiring expert witnesses, and conducting depositions. These costs are typically advanced by your attorney and deducted from your portion of any settlement or award.
- **Medical liens:** If your medical treatment was covered by health insurance or workers' compensation, those entities may have a lien on any settlement or award you receive. Your attorney will work to negotiate these liens to ensure that you receive the maximum amount possible.
- **Taxes:** Depending on the specific nature of your settlement or award, you may owe taxes on some or all the amount you receive. Your attorney can help you understand the tax implications of your case and refer you to a tax professional for guidance.

Always discuss the potential costs of your case with your attorney upfront and ensure you clearly understand how these costs will be handled. Your attorney should provide regular updates on the costs incurred in your case and work with you to make strategic decisions about allocating resources.

While the cost of pursuing a TBI lawsuit can be significant, remember that the goal is to secure the compensation and support you need to move forward with your life and recover from your injuries. With the help of an experienced TBI attorney, you can make informed decisions about your case and work toward achieving the best possible outcome for you and your family.

# 8

# SECURING COMPENSATION AND BENEFITS

**A Pedestrian's Fight for Justice After a Devastating TBI**

The case of Laura F. is a powerful example of the life-altering consequences of a traumatic brain injury caused by a negligent driver. On November 18, 2015, Laura was walking to her bus stop on her way to work when she was struck by a taxi in Contra Costa County, California.[1]

The impact was devastating. Laura's face slammed onto the hood of the car. She suffered a broken mandible, lost six teeth, and was carried approximately thirty feet on the hood of the car before sliding off onto the ground, face down and unresponsive. The responding police officer found her lying in a pool of blood, surrounded by several of her teeth.

Laura was rushed to the hospital, where she underwent emergency surgery to repair her shattered jaw. Her mouth was wired shut, and she was released the following day to begin the long and painful road to recovery. The physical injuries alone were

---

1. https://juryverdictalert.com/vehicles-vs-pedestrian/pedestrian-hit-by-taxi-driver

extensive: a jaw broken in three places, six lost teeth, neck and back injuries, damage to both knees, and a ruptured eardrum. However, the most significant and life-changing injury Laura suffered was a traumatic brain injury.

MRIs of Laura's brain revealed white matter gliosis scars, consistent with axonal shearing—a hallmark of TBI. Expert testimony from Dr. Murray Solomon highlighted the significance of the 7.9% FA Value asymmetry in Laura's brain scans. It noted that such asymmetry was greater than three standard deviations from the mean, indicating a less than 1% chance that it was a normal finding.

Despite the overwhelming evidence of Laura's injuries, the defendant and his insurance company refused to take responsibility for the harm they had caused. They contested the extent of Laura's injuries, particularly the TBI. They even dared to claim that any mental health issues stemmed from preexisting conditions rather than the trauma inflicted by their negligence.

Faced with mounting medical bills and the prospect of a lifetime of disability, Laura and her attorneys refused to back down. They fought tirelessly to hold the driver and his insurance company. At trial, a parade of expert witnesses took the stand to testify about the severity and permanence of Laura's injuries. Specialists in neurosurgery, neurology, neuropsychology, life care planning, neuroradiology, orthopedic surgery, oral surgery, and more painted a vivid picture of the challenges Laura would face for the rest of her life due to the negligence of one inattentive driver.

The trial lasted two weeks, and the jury deliberated for one day. In the end, the jury saw through the defendant's attempts to minimize Laura's suffering and awarded her, by a vote of 12-0, a staggering $5,143,141 in damages. This sum included $100,480 for past medical expenses, $2,042,161 for future medical care, and $3,000,000 for past and future non-economic damages - a testament to this incident's profound impact on every aspect of Laura's life. Her case is a stark reminder of the importance of holding negligent drivers accountable and fighting for the rights of TBI survivors. The award underscores the importance of having experienced, knowledgeable attorneys navigating the complex medical, legal, and financial issues involved in these cases.

**The Financial Impact**

The financial impact of a TBI can be substantial, from mounting medical bills and lost wages to the ongoing costs of rehabilitation and long-term care.

As an experienced TBI attorney, my goal is to help clients navigate this complex landscape. In this chapter, I'll explore the various aspects of securing compensation and benefits after a TBI, from negotiating with insurance companies to structuring settlements for long-term financial stability. I'll also discuss the importance of accessing government benefits and support services that can help ease the financial burden of a TBI. Throughout this chapter, I'll share real-world examples and insights from my experience advocating for TBI survivors and their families.

**Negotiating with Insurance Companies**

Negotiating with insurance companies is one of the first and most critical steps in securing compensation after a TBI. Whether you're dealing with your own insurance provider or the at-fault party's insurer, the process can be complex, time-consuming, and emotionally draining.

Insurance companies are in the business of making money, and their primary goal is to minimize the amount they pay out in claims. They may use a variety of tactics to undervalue your claim or deny it altogether, such as:

- Requesting excessive or unnecessary documentation

- Delaying the processing of your claim
- Disputing the severity or causation of your injuries
- Offering a lowball settlement that doesn't adequately account for your damages

As a TBI attorney, my job is to level the playing field and ensure that the insurance company treats my clients fairly. I do this by:

- Thoroughly investigating your case and gathering all relevant evidence, including police reports, medical records, and witness statements.
- Working with medical experts to establish the extent and long-term impact of your TBI.
- Calculating the total value of your economic and non-economic damages, including future medical expenses, lost earning capacity, pain and suffering, and loss of enjoyment of life.
- Presenting a compelling demand package to the insurance company that outlines the strength of your case and the full extent of your damages.
- Engaging in aggressive negotiation to secure the best possible settlement offer.
- Being prepared to file a lawsuit and take your case to trial if the insurance company refuses to make a fair offer.

In my considerable experience, I know that an insurance company's initial settlement offer is rarely their best offer. They may start with a lowball figure in the hopes that you'll accept it out of desperation or a lack of understanding of the true value of your claim. That's why it's crucial to have an experienced TBI attorney on your side who can advise you on the fairness of any settlement offer.

Sometimes, the insurance company may use underhanded

tactics to undermine your claim. For example, they may hire private investigators to conduct surveillance on you to catch you engaging in activities inconsistent with your claimed injuries. They may also try to use your social media posts or other public statements against you.

My duty as a TBI attorney is to help my clients navigate these challenges and protect client rights throughout the negotiation process. I communicate with the insurance company on your behalf, shielding you from their tactics and allowing you to focus on your recovery. I also advise you on how to protect your privacy and avoid making any statements that could be used against you.

The goal of negotiation is to reach a settlement that fairly compensates you for all your past and future damages, including:

- **Medical expenses**, including hospital bills, surgery costs, and ongoing rehabilitation and therapy.
- **Lost wages and earning capacity** if your TBI has prevented you from working or has limited your ability to earn a living in the future.
- **Pain and suffering**, including the physical pain, emotional distress, and mental anguish caused by your injuries.
- **Loss of enjoyment of life** if your TBI has prevented you from participating in activities you once enjoyed or has diminished your quality of life,
- **Punitive damages** in cases where the at-fault party's conduct was particularly egregious or reckless.

While no amount of money can fully compensate someone for the impact of a TBI on a life, a fair settlement can provide the financial security and peace of mind to move forward. It can help ensure access to the best possible medical care and support services and that no one is left struggling to make ends meet while focusing on recovery.

In the next section, I'll discuss how to structure a settlement to ensure long-term financial stability and protect your eligibility for important government benefits. I'll also explore some real-world examples of TBI settlements and the factors that went into determining the final compensation amount.

## Structuring Settlements for Long-Term Financial Stability

When you receive a settlement from an insurance company or a court award in a TBI case, it's essential to consider how to manage those funds to ensure your long-term financial stability. A well-structured settlement can provide a steady income stream to cover your ongoing medical expenses, replace lost wages, and support your overall quality of life.

One of the first things I consider when structuring a settlement is whether to receive the funds in a lump sum or as a structured settlement. A lump-sum payment gives you immediate access to the full amount of your compensation, which can be helpful if you have significant upfront expenses, such as paying off medical debt or making home modifications to accommodate your injuries.

However, a structured settlement spreads your payments over time and offers several advantages. It can help ensure that you have a reliable source of income for years to come and can protect your funds from being depleted too quickly due to poor financial decisions or unexpected expenses.

Structured settlements can be customized to meet a client's unique needs and goals. I work with financial experts to create a payment schedule that aligns with projected expenses, such as ongoing medical care, rehabilitation, and living costs. We can also build flexibility to account for changes in condition or circumstances over time.

Another factor to consider when structuring a settlement is the impact on your eligibility for government benefits, such as Medicaid or Supplemental Security Income (SSI). A large lump-sum settlement can disqualify you from these needs-based programs, leaving you without access to vital healthcare and financial support.

To avoid this problem, I often recommend establishing a special needs trust to manage your settlement funds. A special needs trust is a legal arrangement that allows you to use your settlement money to pay for essential expenses, such as medical care and housing, without affecting your eligibility for public benefits.

The trust is managed by a trustee, who is responsible for distributing funds according to the terms of the trust and ensuring that the money is used for your benefit. This arrangement can provide peace of mind, knowing that your settlement funds will be used wisely and that you'll have access to the support you need over the long term.

In addition to structuring your settlement payments and protecting your eligibility for benefits, I would counsel you to consider the tax implications of your compensation. In general, settlements for physical injuries, including TBIs, are not taxable under federal law. However, exceptions exist, such as if you claimed a tax deduction for medical expenses related to your injury in a prior year.

I work with tax professionals to ensure that a settlement is structured in the most tax-efficient manner possible and to help clients understand any potential tax liabilities. By taking a proactive approach to tax planning, we can help maximize the long-term value of a settlement and ensure the resources to support recovery and quality of life.

**Accessing Government Benefits and Support Services**

Navigating the complex web of government benefits and support services can be a daunting task for anyone. Still, it's incredibly challenging when you're dealing with the aftermath of a traumatic brain injury (TBI). As an experienced TBI attorney, I've seen firsthand how accessing these resources can make a tremendous difference in the lives of survivors and their families.

One of the first steps I recommend to my clients is to contact their state's brain injury association or alliance. These organizations can provide valuable information and referrals to local resources, such as support groups, rehabilitation providers, and community-based services. They can also help you understand your rights and advocate for your needs within the healthcare and social service systems.

Another resource for TBI survivors is the Social Security Administration (SSA). If your injury has left you unable to work, you may be eligible for Social Security Disability Insurance (SSDI) or Supplemental Security Income (SSI). These programs provide monthly cash benefits to help cover your living expenses and can also grant access to Medicare or Medicaid for your healthcare needs.

However, the application process for Social Security benefits can be complex and time-consuming, and many initial claims are denied. That's where having an experienced disability attorney can make a significant difference. I work closely with my clients to gather the necessary medical evidence, complete the application forms, and present the strongest case to the SSA. If a claim is denied, I can also represent clients in the appeals process to fight for the benefits they deserve.

In addition to Social Security benefits, a variety of other government programs can provide financial and practical support to TBI survivors and their families. These may include:

- **Vocational rehabilitation services,** which can help you retrain for a new job or adapt to your current job with accommodations.
- **Housing assistance programs,** which can help you find and afford accessible housing.
- **Transportation services,** which can provide rides to medical appointments and other essential errands.

- **Respite care services,** which can provide temporary relief for family caregivers.
- **Personal care assistance,** which can help with activities of daily living such as bathing, dressing, and eating.

Accessing these services requires navigating a complex bureaucracy and meeting specific eligibility criteria. I help clients understand the options and connect them with the appropriate agencies and organizations to get needed support.

Remember that government benefits and support services are never a substitute for the compensation you may be entitled to through a legal claim against the party responsible for your injury. However, they can provide a vital lifeline during the legal process and beyond, helping to ease the financial burden and ensure you have access to the care and resources you need to maximize your recovery.

## Address the Financial Implications of Inadequate Concussion Care

One of the most significant challenges faced by individuals who have suffered a traumatic brain injury (TBI) is the potential for inadequate or insufficient medical care. When a TBI is not correctly diagnosed, treated, or managed, it can lead to long-term physical, cognitive, and emotional consequences that can profoundly impact a person's quality of life and financial well-being.

Some of the common financial implications of inadequate care include:

- **Lost income and earning capacity:** If your symptoms persist or worsen due to improper care, you may be unable to return to work or experience a reduced earning capacity over time. This situation can result in

significant lost wages and income, which can be difficult to recover without proper legal representation.
- **Out-of-pocket medical expenses:** Seeking specialized care, such as seeing a neurologist or undergoing cognitive rehabilitation therapy, can be expensive and may not be fully covered by insurance. You may be responsible for substantial out-of-pocket costs that can strain your finances and impact your ability to access the care you need.
- **Long-term disability and care needs:** In severe cases, inadequate care can lead to permanent disabilities that require ongoing medical treatment, assistive devices, and personal care services. Long-term needs can be astronomically expensive and may not be fully covered by insurance or government benefits.
- **Reduced quality of life:** A poorly managed TBI's physical, cognitive, and emotional effects can take a significant toll on your overall quality of life. You may be unable to participate in activities you once enjoyed, experience strained relationships with loved ones, and face various other challenges that can be difficult to quantify financially.

When I work with clients, one of my primary goals is to ensure they have access to the medical care and support services they need to maximize their recovery. I have witnessed the devastating impact that inadequate TBI care can have on my clients' lives and finances. My firm will connect them with top medical specialists, advocate for their insurance coverage, and pursue every available legal action against the parties responsible for their injury.

I also work closely with medical and financial experts to fully assess the long-term costs and implications of my client's TBI. By taking a comprehensive approach to valuing the economic consequences of a TBI, I can help my clients secure generous compensation. My goal is always to give them the financial security and peace of mind they'll need for their journey of recovery.

## The Importance of Working with a Top Law Firm

When it comes to securing compensation for the long-term effects of a traumatic brain injury (TBI), having a skilled and experienced legal professional can make a significant difference in the outcome of your case. While it may be tempting to try and venture into the legal system on your own or settle for a less experienced attorney, doing so can have severe consequences for your financial future and overall well-being.

At my own firm, Hackard Law, we bring over forty years of experience to every TBI case we handle. This depth of knowledge allows us to navigate the complex medical, legal, and financial issues involved in these cases and build strong, compelling claims for our clients. Throughout my years of experience as a TBI attorney, I have identified the hallmarks of firms that achieve the best possible outcomes for their clients:

- An extensive network of medical and financial experts. These professionals provide critical insight and testimony that can be invaluable in supporting your claim and demonstrating the full extent of your damages.
- Highly personalized approach to each case. The best firms work closely with clients to understand their unique needs and goals. They craft targeted legal strategies tailored to specific circumstances, maximizing the chances of success.
- Passion for fighting for the rights of TBI survivors and their families. Brain injuries are life altering. Successful firms are dedicated to helping clients secure the resources they need to rebuild their lives.

Powerful opponents, such as large insurance companies or corporations, don't intimidate me. Decades of advocacy have left their mark - I am always prepared to fight for client rights in court if necessary. My goal is to provide the skilled counsel and personalized support my clients need to navigate the legal process and achieve the best possible outcome. Our clients have total confidence that a strong, experienced legal team is on their side, fighting for their rights every step of the way.

# 9

# THE ROLE OF FAMILY AND CAREGIVERS IN TBI RECOVERY

**A Mother's Story**

When a loved one suffers a traumatic brain injury (TBI), the impact reverberates throughout the entire family. Over decades representing injured plaintiffs, I've seen firsthand how critical the role of family and caregivers is in the recovery process. It's not just about supporting the individual with TBI through the legal journey; it's about being there for them every step of the way, from finding the right medical care to coping with the emotional and psychological fallout of the injury.

The story of Dixie and her son Paul is a powerful example of the difference that dedicated family support can make in the life of a TBI survivor. In her poignant account, "TBI Ten Years Later: A Mother's Story Continues,"[1] Dixie shares both the triumphs and ongoing struggles she and her family have faced since Paul sustained a severe TBI in an accident at age thirteen.

When Paul was first injured, the Coskie family had to suddenly become his advocates, fighting for the best possible

---

1. https://www.brainline.org/story/tbi-ten-years-later-mothers-story-continues

medical care, rehabilitation services, and educational accommodations. They had to traverse a complex web of insurance claims, legal proceedings, and bureaucratic hurdles while trying to maintain some sense of normalcy for their other seven children.

As Paul slowly emerged from a coma and began the long, grueling process of rehabilitation, his family was there beside him every step of the way. They participated in therapy sessions, learned how to provide home nursing care, and adapted their home to accommodate Paul's new needs. They celebrated every small victory, from the first time he blinked his eyes to the day he took his first unsteady steps.

But the journey was far from over. As Paul transitioned back to school and eventually graduated, the Coskies had to continue advocating for his needs, working with neuropsychologists and special education teams to develop an individualized education plan (IEP) to help him succeed. They also had to grapple with the social and emotional impact of the injury, as Paul's friends drifted away, and his personality underwent subtle but significant changes.

Even as Paul made remarkable progress, learning to walk and talk again, volunteering at the hospital where his life was saved, and even attending college, the scars of the TBI remained. Dixie writes, "Despite all the miraculous gains my son has made over the years, my heart often remains heavy. When I look into my husband's or my children's eyes, I can still see the lingering fear, the permanent scars."

The Coskie family's story is a testament to the incredible resilience and love that families of TBI survivors must draw upon in the face of unimaginable challenges. It's also a reminder of how vital it is for these families to access the resources, support, and legal advocacy they need to help their loved ones thrive.

**Fighting for the Family**

At my firm, we understand that when we take on a TBI case, we're not just representing an individual client; we're fighting for the well-being of an entire family. We work closely with our clients and their caregivers to ensure that they have the tools and resources they need to navigate the legal process, access top-quality medical care and rehabilitation services, and rebuild their lives in the wake of a devastating injury.

We also recognize the profound emotional and psychological impact that a TBI can have on family members and caregivers. The grief, fear, and exhaustion that come with supporting a loved one through recovery can be overwhelming, and caregivers need to have their own support systems in place. That's why we strive to be more than just legal advocates; we aim to provide compassion, understanding, and hope for the families we serve.

With the right support, resources, and legal representation, it is possible to prevail in even the most daunting struggles and build a fulfilling life in the wake of a traumatic injury. As Dixie's story shows, the road may be long and difficult, but with the love and dedication of family and caregivers, there is always reason to hope.

**Supporting a Loved One with TBI Through the Legal Process**

When a family member suffers a traumatic brain injury, navigating the legal system can feel like an overwhelming burden on top of an already difficult situation. However, understanding the legal implications of TBI and having the proper support can make a significant difference in ensuring a loved one's long-term well-being and financial security.

Choosing top legal representation is one of the first steps in supporting your loved one. Look for an attorney who has experience in handling TBI cases and demonstrates empathy, patience, and a willingness to take the time to understand your family's unique needs and concerns. A good attorney will act as both a legal advocate and a source of support during this challenging time.

As a family member, you can play a vital role in gathering evidence and documentation to support your loved one's case. Supporting evidence may include keeping detailed records of medical appointments, therapy sessions, and any out-of-pocket expenses related to the injury. You may also be asked to provide information about your loved one's pre-injury lifestyle, work history, and relationships to help demonstrate the extent of the losses suffered.

Be prepared for the emotional challenges that can arise during the legal process. Depositions and court appearances can be stressful and may require you to relive painful memories or confront difficult realities about your loved one's condition. Lean on your support system, and don't hesitate to seek professional counseling if needed to help you cope with the emotional toll of the process.

Regarding settlement negotiations and awards, do your best to understand your loved one's long-term needs and priorities clearly. An experienced attorney can help you evaluate settlement offers and ensure that any award considers future medical expenses, lost earning potential, and other very long-term considerations. If they have the skills, your attorney can also assist with setting up trusts or other financial management tools to protect your loved one's assets and meet their care needs. If not, I strongly advise you to seek a trust and estate attorney.

Throughout the legal process, remember that your role as a family member is not just to serve as a source of information or to make decisions on your loved one's behalf. You are also there to provide emotional support, encouragement, and a sense of stability during a time of upheaval. Celebrate the small victories along the way and remind your loved one that the outcome of any legal proceeding does not define their worth.

By approaching the legal process with patience, persistence, and a focus on your loved one's well-being, you can help ensure that they receive the support they need to move forward with their lives after a traumatic brain injury. Take advantage of every opportunity to consult with professionals and avail yourself of the many resources mentioned in this book that can help guide you every step.

## Finding the Right Medical Care and Rehabilitation Services

The quality and appropriateness of the care someone receives after a TBI can profoundly impact their long-term health, functioning, and quality of life. As a family member or caregiver, you play an essential role in helping to navigate the complex healthcare system and advocating for your loved one's needs.

When it comes to medical care, seek out providers who have specific experience and expertise in treating TBI. They will likely include neurologists, neurosurgeons, rehabilitation physicians, neuropsychologists, and other specialists who understand the unique challenges and needs of individuals with brain injuries. Never hesitate to ask questions about a provider's qualifications, experience, and approach to treatment before deciding. Professionals sporting a long list of academic credentials can seem intimidating, but remember that they are just people like you.

One of the keys to effective TBI treatment is a comprehensive, coordinated approach that addresses the full range of an individual's needs. Depending on the complexity of a case, such treatments may involve a combination of medical interventions, such as medication management and surgical procedures, as well as rehabilitation therapies, such as physical therapy, occupational therapy, speech therapy, and cognitive rehabilitation. The goal is to help your loved one regain as much function and independence as possible while also addressing any ongoing symptoms or challenges.

When evaluating rehabilitation programs, look for ones that offer a multidisciplinary team approach, with professionals from different specialties working collaboratively to develop and implement an individualized treatment plan. The program should also have experience working with individuals with TBIs and offer various services and technologies to promote recovery and adaptation. Based on their prior experiences, your attorney may be a good referral resource.

Also, the setting and intensity of the rehabilitation program should be considered. Some individuals may require inpatient rehabilitation in a specialized facility, especially in the early stages of recovery or if they have complex medical needs. Others may benefit from outpatient or community-based programs that allow them to receive therapy while living at home. If you can, look for a program matching your loved one's needs and goals.

In addition to formal rehabilitation programs, there are many community resources and support services that can be invaluable in helping individuals with TBI and their families tackle the challenges of recovery. Searching on Google or Facebook can lead to brain injury support groups, vocational rehabilitation programs, assistive technology services, and respite care for caregivers. Never be afraid to reach out and ask for help – many organizations and professionals are dedicated to supporting individuals and families affected by TBIs.

As you explore medical care and rehabilitation options, keep in mind the long-term nature of TBI recovery. While many individuals make significant progress in the early stages of treatment, the recovery journey can extend for months, years, or even a lifetime. Ongoing communication with your loved one's healthcare team can help you prepare and adjust treatment plans and goals as needed over time.

My most important advice is never to hesitate to ask questions, express concerns, or advocate for your loved one's needs. Trust your instincts, and don't fear seeking a second opinion if something doesn't feel right. By actively participating in your loved one's care and working collaboratively with their healthcare providers, you can help ensure they receive the best treatment and support on their recovery journey.

## Coping with the Emotional and Psychological Impact of TBI

The sudden and profound changes brought about by TBI can trigger a complex range of emotions, from fear and anxiety to grief, anger, and depression. As a family member or caregiver, recognize these feelings as a normal and valid response to a challenging situation.

One of the most potent emotions many families experience in the wake of a TBI is grief. Even if your loved one survives the injury, you may find yourself mourning the loss of the person you knew before the accident. Instead of bottling it up, allow yourself to experience and express this grief. Acknowledge that the path forward may be different than the one you had envisioned and permit yourself to feel the pain of that loss.

At the same time, try to maintain a sense of hope and perspective. Recovery from a TBI is a journey, not a destination, and that progress can continue for months or even years after the initial injury. Celebrate the small victories along the way, and focus on the strengths and resilience of your loved one rather than dwelling on the challenges.

In my experience, it is common for family members and caregivers to experience feelings of guilt, self-blame, or helplessness in the aftermath of a TBI. You may find yourself second-guessing decisions you made leading up to the accident or feeling like you're not doing enough to support your loved one's recovery. It may be hard to set them aside, but such feelings are not productive. Remind yourself that you are doing the best you can in a tough situation and that taking care of your own needs is okay.

One helpful framework for understanding the emotional journey of TBI recovery is the stages of grief, as described by Elisabeth Kübler-Ross. While not everyone experiences these stages in the same order or intensity, they can provide a roadmap for the common emotional responses to loss and change.

The five stages are:

1. **Denial:** In the initial shock of a TBI diagnosis, it's common to experience feelings of disbelief or numbness. You may think, "This can't be happening," or "There must be some mistake."
2. **Anger:** As the reality of the situation sinks in, you may feel intense anger or frustration. This anger may be directed at the person responsible for the injury, healthcare providers, or the world.
3. **Bargaining:** In this stage, you may find yourself making deals with a higher power or with fate, thinking things like, "If only my loved one recovers, I promise to be a better person."
4. **Depression:** As you begin to grapple with the long-term implications of the injury, feelings of sadness, hopelessness, and despair are common. You may feel like life will never be the same or that you'll never be able to find joy or purpose again.
5. **Acceptance:** Over time, you may begin to find peace and acceptance with the new reality of your situation. Acceptance doesn't mean you're happy about what happened, but that you've found a way to adapt and move forward.

Note that the stages are not linear, and moving back and forth between them is common over time. Be patient with yourself and your emotional process, and don't hesitate to seek support from friends, family, or mental health professionals.

As a countermeasure to the five stages of grief, I'd like to suggest five strategies to help cope with the emotional and psychological impact of TBI:

1. **Practice self-care:** Take care of your physical, emotional, and mental health needs. Get enough rest, eat well, exercise, and engage in activities that bring you joy and relaxation.
2. **Seek support:** Don't try to shoulder the burden of caregiving alone. Contact friends, family members, or support groups for help and emotional support. Consider seeking professional counseling or therapy to help you process your feelings and develop coping strategies.
3. **Communicate openly:** Be honest with your loved one and other family members about your feelings and needs. Encourage open and honest communication within the family and be willing to listen to others' perspectives and emotions as well.
4. **Find meaning and purpose:** Look for ways to find meaning and purpose in your experience, whether through advocating for TBI awareness, supporting other families, or finding personal growth and resilience in the face of adversity.
5. **Practice gratitude:** Even during difficult circumstances, try to find things to be grateful for. Gratefulness may include the support of loved ones, the skill and compassion of healthcare providers, or the small moments of joy and progress in your loved one's recovery.

**The Impact of a TBI on Family Relationships and Dynamics**

A traumatic brain injury is not just a life-altering event for the individual who suffers the injury but also for the entire family system. The sudden and profound changes brought about by TBI often and usually disrupt established family roles, routines, and dynamics, creating new stressors for everyone involved.

A shift in roles and responsibilities is one of the most significant changes many families experience after a TBI. The injured individual may no longer be able to fulfill their previous roles as a provider, parent, or partner, leading other family members to take on new tasks and responsibilities. This situation can be daunting for spouses or partners who suddenly find themselves in the role of primary caregiver, balancing the demands of their loved one's care with their own needs and responsibilities.

Children and siblings of individuals with a TBI may also struggle with the changes in their family structure and dynamics. They may feel neglected or overlooked as the focus of the family shifts to the injured individual, or they may struggle with feelings of guilt, anger, or confusion about their loved one's condition. Families must make a concerted effort to maintain open lines of communication and to provide support and reassurance to all members during this challenging time.

Another typical challenge families face after a TBI is changes in personality or behavior in the injured individual. Depending on the location and severity of the injury, individuals with TBI may experience changes in mood, impulse control, or social behavior that can strain family relationships. They may become easily frustrated or agitated or struggle with disinhibition or inappropriate social conduct. Families may need to learn new communication and conflict resolution strategies to maintain positive relationships in the face of these trials.

TBI also has severe and often detrimental effects on marital and romantic relationships. Spouses or partners of individuals with a TBI may struggle with feelings of loss or grief for the relationship they once had, as well as new challenges related to intimacy, communication, and changing roles within the relationship. Seeking support from counselors or therapists working with couples affected by TBI can be important in maintaining and strengthening these relationships over time.

I often counsel caregivers that their job can be emotionally and physically demanding. They must take breaks, seek respite care, and maintain their physical and mental health. Engaging in family activities and rituals, seeking support from friends and community resources, and maintaining a sense of normalcy and routine can all promote family well-being in the face of a TBI.

No one is ever prepared when a loved one suffers a traumatic brain injury. How could you be? Acknowledge that there will be bad days, weeks, and possibly years ahead. Try to understand that grief has stages and that finding meaning in adversity is as essential for you as it is for the TBI victim. The recovery process will be long and arduous, but you may find unexpected strength when needed. The journey of TBI recovery is not one that any individual or family should have to take alone. Seek out the most experienced medical, legal, spiritual, and other support professionals you can find.

The good news is that I'm here to tell you that by drawing on the love, strength, and resilience of the family, individuals and families affected by a TBI can and do find hope, healing, and a path forward together. Your life and the lives of everyone in your family will never be the same, but you may still find joy, peace, and happiness.

The journey of a family affected by TBI is a long and challenging one, but it is not without optimism. Ten years after her son suffered a devastating TBI, Dixie, the mother we met at the beginning of this chapter, offered the following about her situation and the advice she would give to others, words I wholeheartedly agree with:

"Ten years later, my heart also remains heavy as I think of other families who will receive the unthinkable news that one of their loved ones has sustained a life-altering injury. I understand all too well the grief and uphill battles they are sure to encounter. I also pray that these families will reach out to get help and resources, to have the strength and will to advocate, to never give up ... and to keep hope alive."

# 10

# MANAGING THE FINANCIAL IMPLICATIONS OF TBI

### Khalia's Story

Khalia Carter, a high school senior from Fort Myers, Florida, had her life turned upside down when, driving home one evening after spending time with friends, a drunk motorcyclist three times over the legal limit hit her car on April 18, 2022.[1] The crash left Khalia with a severe traumatic brain injury (TBI) that affected her ability to walk, speak, and perform daily tasks independently. As Khalia embarked on her journey of recovery and rehabilitation, her family faced not only the emotional and physical challenges of adapting to their new reality, but also the daunting financial burden that comes with treating a TBI.

The costs associated with TBI treatment can be staggering. According to Next Avenue, a PBS-affiliated non-profit journal, in 2016 the average lifetime cost of medical treatment for a person with a severe TBI ranged from $85,000 to $3 million.[2] Consid-

---

1. https://www.hopkinsmedicine.org/health/conditions-and-diseases/traumatic-brain-injury/patient-story-khalia
2. https://www.nextavenue.org/the-steep-cost-of-brain-injury-recovery/

the escalating healthcare costs since then, a current estimate would be two to three times higher. Expenses such as emergency medical care, hospitalizations, surgeries, rehabilitation, and long-term support services are exorbitantly expensive.

For Khalia and her family, the immediate costs they faced, included:

- Emergency room treatment and diagnostic tests.
- Intensive care unit (ICU) stay.
- Neurosurgery to address brain swelling.
- Inpatient rehabilitation.
- Medications and medical equipment.

Fortunately for her, Khalia's mother worked at Johns Hopkins Medical Center, where her daughter could receive world-class medical treatment. Presumably, her mother's health insurance also covered a portion of her immediate expenses, but others are not so lucky. Families often find themselves responsible for significant out-of-pocket costs, such as deductibles, copayments, and uncovered services. In many cases, a TBI victim or the family could end up paying thousands or even tens of thousands of dollars before catastrophic insurance coverage would kick in.

Consider also that a family like Khalia's may face many indirect costs that are seldom and, in some cases, never covered by insurance, such as:

- Lost wages due to time off work to care for Khalia.
- Travel costs to and from medical appointments.
- Home modifications to accommodate Khalia's mobility needs.
- Assistive technology and adaptive equipment.

Such expenses, always unplanned, add significant financial strain on families coping with the emotional and logistical strains of caring for a loved one with a TBI.

The biggest unknown in TBI cases is the long-term costs from problems and symptoms that might not occur for years. Recent video interviews show that Khalia has made great progress in regaining her independence and relearning basic skills like walking. Nevertheless, victims in her situation often require ongoing physical, occupational, and speech therapy. They also sometimes need additional surgeries, medications, or assistive devices as recovery progresses. Ongoing expenses can extend for a decade or more after the initial injury.

**Hope for the Best, But Plan for the Worst**

In cases like Khalia's, where another party's negligence or wrongdoing caused the injury, pursuing legal action may be necessary to secure the compensation needed to cover the full spectrum of costs associated with the TBI. A proficient TBI attorney can help families understand their legal rights, navigate the complex claims process, and fight for the resources they need to ensure the best possible outcome for their loved ones.

While no amount of money can erase the aftermath of a TBI, securing fair compensation can help alleviate the financial burden on families, allowing them to focus on what matters most: supporting their loved one's recovery and rebuilding their lives in the wake of a devastating injury.

As we explore the various aspects of managing the financial implications of TBI in this chapter, keep in mind the real-world impact of these injuries on survivors and their families. It's never easy to predict the long-term course of a TBI, which means that we always hope for the best, but we plan for the worst. By understanding the scope of the costs involved and the importance of proactive financial planning and legal advocacy, we can work to ensure that families like Khalia's have the resources and support they need to weather the storm and emerge stronger on the other side.

The first advice I give every client who consults me about a TBI case is: brace yourself. The financial impact of a traumatic brain injury can be staggering, with costs extending far beyond initial medical treatment. Consider that emergency medical care, hospitalizations, surgeries, and rehabilitation services may be just the tip of the iceberg. The cost of inpatient rehabilitation can vary widely, with some facilities charging thousands of dollars per day. Families often need to purchase assistive technology or adaptive equipment for ongoing care, which can add considerably to the financial burden. Long-term care costs can accumulate rapidly, especially if the individual requires ongoing therapy sessions, specialized transportation, or home modifications to accommodate mobility needs. It can be overwhelming, I know, but don't be discouraged. I'll guide you step-by-step through all the big issues.

## Understanding Insurance Coverage and Medical Expenses

Understanding your insurance coverage and the potential out-of-pocket expenses you may face is a first step in navigating the complex landscape of TBI care. I've witnessed many families' confusion and frustration when trying to make sense of their insurance policies and medical bills. It's common for people to assume that their insurance will cover all their expenses, only to be blindsided by high deductibles, copayments, or denied claims.

Step one in managing the financial impact of a TBI is to review your health insurance policy carefully. Look for information on coverage for emergency care, hospitalization, rehabilitation, and long-term care. Pay close attention to any limits on coverage, such as annual or lifetime maximums, and any exclusions or restrictions on the types of services covered.

Insurance contracts are generally not user-friendly. They are sometimes difficult for even attorneys to understand, so I sympathize with my clients who struggle to make heads or tails of them. The crucial sections to look at are the out-of-pocket responsibilities, which may include deductibles (the amount you must pay before your insurance coverage kicks in), copayments (a fixed amount you pay for each medical service), and coinsurance (a percentage of the cost of each service that you're responsible for). These costs can add up quickly, especially if your loved one requires extensive or ongoing care.

Understanding your health insurance policy—determining what is covered and what is not—should be among your top priorities. Standard exclusions or limitations include limits on the number of therapy sessions, restrictions on certain treatments, and caps on coverage for specific types of care. Also, some insurance policies may require pre-approval for specific therapies, complicating the process.

In addition to health insurance, it's worth exploring other potential sources of coverage or financial assistance. For example, suppose the TBI was caused by a car accident. In that case, your auto insurance policy may include medical payment coverage or personal injury protection to help cover some costs. If the injury occurred on the job, workers' compensation may cover medical expenses and lost wages.

From the very start of this odyssey, do your very best to keep detailed records of all medical expenses related to the TBI, including bills, receipts, and insurance statements. Such documentation will be essential if you must file an insurance claim, appeal a denied claim, or pursue legal action to recover damages.

One thing to keep in mind is that even if you have good insurance coverage, you may still face significant out-of-pocket costs related to your loved one's TBI care. An attorney who regularly deals with insurance companies can help you explore all potential sources of compensation.

. . .

Managing the financial impact of a TBI requires a proactive, informed approach. Don't be afraid to ask questions, seek guidance, and advocate for your loved one's needs. With the right support and resources, you can focus on what matters most: helping your loved one recover and rebuild their life after a devastating injury.

Here are a few key takeaways to keep in mind:

- Review your health insurance policy carefully to understand your coverage and out-of-pocket responsibilities.
- Explore other potential coverage or financial assistance sources, such as auto insurance, workers' compensation, or government benefits.
- Keep detailed records of all medical expenses related to the TBI, including bills, receipts, and insurance statements.
- Work with a law firm that wants to help you understand your legal rights and options and will advocate with insurance companies and other parties on your behalf. You need a representative who is willing to fight for you.
- Don't be afraid to ask for help or guidance as you navigate the complex and often overwhelming world of TBI care and finances.

At my own firm, Hackard Law, we know that when it comes to TBI cases, there is no 'normal' or 'standard' anything. Each case is as unique as the TBI victim. Because the complexities are daunting and our client's needs always come first, we are here to help them every step of the way.

## Planning for Long-Term Care Needs

While it can be difficult to contemplate the future during a crisis, taking a proactive approach to long-term care planning can help ensure that your loved one receives the support and resources they need to achieve the best possible outcome. One of the first things to understand about TBI is that the road to recovery is often long and unpredictable. Some individuals may make significant progress in the early stages of treatment, but others may require ongoing care and support for months, years, or even a lifetime. For this reason, you'll want a team of medical professionals to help you assess your loved one's unique needs and develop a comprehensive plan for their care.

This plan may include a range of services and supports, such as:

- **Rehabilitation:** Many individuals with TBI require extensive rehabilitation to help them regain lost skills and abilities. Rehab may include physical therapy to improve mobility and strength, occupational therapy to help with daily living activities, and speech therapy to address communication and swallowing difficulties.
- **Assistive technology:** Depending on the severity of the injury, your loved one may benefit from assistive devices or technology to help them navigate their environment and communicate with others. Assistance can include everything from simple tools like grab bars and adapted utensils to more advanced devices like voice-activated software or eye-gaze-controlled computers.
- **Home modifications:** If your loved one lives at home, you may need to modify the house to accommodate their needs. Installing ramps or lifts, widening doorways, or remodeling bathrooms to make them

more accessible are just a few options you may want to consider.

- **Personal care assistance:** Many individuals with TBI require help with basic activities of daily living, such as bathing, dressing, and grooming. You may need to hire a personal care attendant or work with a home health agency to provide this support.
- **Ongoing medical care:** TBI can lead to a range of long-term medical issues, such as seizures, chronic pain, or hormonal imbalances. I can't stress enough how important it is to work with a team of medical specialists who can help manage these conditions and prevent complications.
- **Mental health support:** The uncertainty of recovery, coupled with the stress of managing care and finances, can lead to anxiety and depression. Acknowledging these emotions will aid in the healing process. Consider joining a support group.

One of the biggest issues in planning for long-term care is figuring out how to pay for it. The costs of TBI care can be staggering, and even the best insurance policies may have gaps or limitations in coverage. Don't be shy about exploring all potential sources of funding and support.

You may also be eligible for government benefits, such as Social Security Disability Insurance (SSDI) or Medicaid, which can help cover some long-term care costs. However, the application process for these programs can be complex and time-consuming, so seek guidance from a qualified professional.

Another aspect of long-term care planning is respecting your loved one's wishes and preferences. You may have to have difficult conversations about advanced directives, power of attorney, and guardianship. While these topics can be uncomfortable to discuss, you must have a clear plan to ensure your loved one's needs and desires are met.

When developing a long-term care plan, prioritize the various services and supports based on your loved one's needs and situation. Some needs, such as ongoing medical care and rehabilitation, may be non-negotiable and require immediate attention. Others, like home modifications or assistive technology, may be important but less urgent. Work with your loved one's medical team and consider their input when determining which services are essential for their recovery and quality of life.

Of course, costs must always be considered. Some, like personal care assistance or home health services, may be covered by insurance or government benefits. In contrast, others, like home modifications or certain types of therapy, may need to be paid for out-of-pocket. When prioritizing needs, consider the immediate and long-term costs and how they fit into your financial plan. It may be helpful to create a budget or work with a financial advisor to determine how to allocate your resources most effectively.

Your loved one's needs may change over time, so it's essential to regularly reassess their situation and adjust the long-term care plan accordingly. By staying flexible and proactive, you can ensure your loved one receives the most appropriate and effective care throughout their recovery journey.

Ultimately, planning for the long-term care needs of a loved one with TBI requires a team effort. It involves working closely with medical professionals, legal experts, financial advisors, and other specialists to create a comprehensive plan that addresses all aspects of your loved one's care. It also involves advocating for your loved one's needs and rights and being willing to ask for help and support when needed.

As someone who has worked with countless families affected by life-threatening injuries, I know firsthand how overwhelming and challenging this process can be. But I also know that with the right information, resources, and support, it is possible to create a plan that helps your loved one live the fullest, most meaningful life possible.

So, if you're facing the daunting task of planning for the long-term care needs of a TBI victim, remember that you're not alone. Reach out to the experts and advocates who can guide you through this process, and don't be afraid to lean on your family, friends, and community for support. With a clear plan and a strong support system, you can help your loved one overcome the challenges of TBI and work toward a better tomorrow.

## The Importance of Working with Experienced Legal and Financial Professionals

Regarding legal matters, having an attorney skilled in TBI cases can make all the difference. Such attorneys know the unique challenges and complexities involved in TBI cases, and they can help you understand your legal rights and options. They can work with you to build a strong case, negotiate with insurance companies, and pursue the compensation you need to cover your loved one's medical expenses, lost wages, and other costs.

But it's not just about the legal expertise. I strongly advise you to work with a firm with staff and attorneys who have a deep compassion and understanding of what you and your family are going through. They should be partners and advocates who listen to your concerns, answer your questions, and fight tirelessly to protect your loved one's interests.

In addition to legal support, working with expert financial professionals is another important consideration. These professionals can help you understand your insurance coverage, explore potential sources of funding and support, and create a long-term financial plan that considers your loved one's ongoing care needs.

For example, a financial advisor specializing in special needs planning can help you navigate the complex world of government benefits, such as Social Security Disability Insurance (SSDI) and Medicaid. They can also help you set up a special needs trust to provide for your loved one's care and support without jeopardizing their eligibility for these important programs.

Working with seasoned professionals can also help you bypass common pitfalls and mistakes that can have serious consequences down the road. For example, an attorney can help you avoid signing away your legal rights in an insurance settlement. Similarly, a financial advisor can help you avoid making investment decisions that could put your loved one's long-term care at risk.

Of course, choose your legal and financial partners carefully. Look for professionals with a track record of success and who take the time to understand your unique needs and goals. Don't be afraid to ask questions, seek referrals, and trust your instincts when finding the right fit.

**Resilience and Determination**

Throughout this chapter, we've explored the financial implications of traumatic brain injury (TBI) and the strategies and resources available to help manage these challenges. We've seen how understanding insurance coverage, planning for long-term care needs, and working with skilled professionals can make a meaningful difference in the lives of TBI survivors and their families.

But perhaps most importantly, we've been reminded of the incredible resilience and determination of those affected by TBI. Khalia's story, which we began with, is a powerful example of this. Despite suffering a devastating injury that left her with a long road to recovery, Khalia set a goal for herself: to walk across the stage at her high school graduation. And with the support of her family, her medical team, and her unwavering spirit, she did just that.

Now, Khalia is enrolled in college, pursuing her dreams, and building a future for herself. Her life may not be the same as it was before her injury, and she may face further obstacles. But she has shown that it is possible to move forward and find a new path with the right support, resources, and mindset.

The same is true for all TBI survivors and their families. The road ahead may be long and difficult, but there is always hope for a brighter future. By taking a proactive approach to managing the financial impact of TBI, seeking out the guidance and support of legal and financial experts, and holding on to the love and resilience of family and community, you can help your loved one stay the course on this journey and emerge stronger on the other side.

Khalia's mother, Shawnda, reminds us, "Khalia pushes through. She has the most positive attitude, and she is such a strong girl, so I know whatever she puts her mind to, she can do it."

May we all find that same strength and positivity in the face of adversity and never lose sight of the hope and possibilities that lie ahead.

# 11

# LIFE AFTER TBI: STORIES OF HOPE AND RESILIENCE

**Dylan's Miraculous Recovery**

It was an average spring day that instantly became a nightmare for nineteen-year-old Dylan. Driving down a sunny road, his whole life ahead of him, Dylan suddenly fell victim to a devastating accident. Emergency responders arrived to find his vehicle crumpled and unrecognizable. It took them eight agonizing minutes to extract Dylan's barely breathing and unresponsive body from the wreckage.[1]

Medical scans revealed Dylan had suffered a diffuse axonal injury - one of the most severe types of traumatic brain injuries, with multiple areas of bleeding in and around his brain. Emergency surgery was required to relieve the mounting pressure and internal bleeding. Dylan's condition remained critical, with doctors fearing he could end up in a permanent vegetative state, severely disabled, or even dead within six months if he survived at all.

Yet, against all odds, a spark of hope emerged seventeen days

---

1. https://www.flintrehab.com/severe-brain-injury-recovery-stories/

later when Dylan's eyes opened spontaneously. This small sign of consciousness marked a turning point on his rocky road to recovery. Dylan slowly transitioned from a coma to a vegetative state and eventually to an inpatient neurorehabilitation program - each incremental step a hard-won victory.

Two months in, Dylan had progressed from being bedridden to moving from bed to chair with moderate assistance. By the three-month mark, in what doctors called a remarkable achievement, he was walking fifty feet independently and accurately responding to yes-or-no questions.

Dylan's resilience and determination shone through at every stage. When his one-year follow-up arrived, the once-grim prognosis had been defied - Dylan had regained his independence, living at home and performing nearly all his daily activities without help.

His journey exemplifies the power of perseverance, world-class rehabilitation, and the incredible plasticity of the human brain and spirit. Dylan's case serves as a beacon of hope, showing that even when the most skilled medical teams deliver devastating predictions based on initial exams and scans, they do not determine the outcome. With intense therapy, an unwavering support system, and an indomitable will to overcome, the impossible can become attainable for survivors of even the most severe traumatic brain injuries.

## Ann's Unstoppable Mission: From Survivor to Savior for 60,000 Brain Injury Victims

On an ordinary day in 1998, Ann's life was altered forever in a split second when a severe car crash left her with a traumatic brain injury - and very little support or guidance for recovering from it. She barely clung to consciousness after the impact, her symptoms rapidly spiraling - swelling in her brain, constant pain, physical complications like a misaligned jaw that would require extensive surgery to repair.[2]

But the invisible wounds haunted her most. Depression, anxiety, paranoia, and cognitive impairments like the inability to write, use a computer, or even remember how to get home from neighborhood routes she once knew like the back of her hand. Her brain injury went undiagnosed for over a year, forcing her to white-knuckle through a confusing, isolating recovery.

As a busy corporate executive and mother of three young children, Ann could not afford to be sidelined. She forced herself through each day, sensing her family's fear, and felt alone in her newfound battles. She got lost constantly, basic multi-tasking was arduous, and simply using a computer felt insurmountable.

When she finally received her brain injury diagnosis over a year later, Ann went home and sobbed at the reality she had been denying. How could she take care of three kids while battling her own debilitating condition? The two shared many symptoms - word-finding issues, crippling fatigue, and post-traumatic stress. However, this connection gave Ann critical insight into her daughter's struggles. She knew when to let her work through aphasia lapses patiently rather than forcing the words. Facing these challenges together became a turning point.

Out of those isolating years grew Ann's life mission - to ensure no brain injury survivor ever felt so alone and cast adrift again. In 2001, she founded the Brain Injury Peer Visitor Association,[3] a nonprofit staffed by a volunteer army of nearly 100 survivors dedicated to providing hope, empathy, and support.

What began as Ann's dream quickly swelled into an unprecedented system of care. Her peer visitors fanned out across hospitals, rehab facilities, and nursing homes, building a remarkable 60,000 supportive connections with patients and families.

---

2. https://www.youtube.com/watch?v=QViCdOEgEXQ
3. https://braininjurypeervisitor.org/

Doctors, mostly skeptical of non-professionals, saw the impact and invited them in.

Ann's innovative model provided something the medical field had been missing - human connection, insight, and first-hand experience from those who had walked the same disorienting path. Her peer visitors gave brain injury survivors and their loved ones a lifeline of empathy from "someone who had been there and done that."

Today, over two decades later, Ann's vision of person-to-person support has transformed glimpses of hope into a future of possibility for tens of thousands across the globe. Her lifetime of turning tragedy into triumph has yielded a legacy of compassion, advocacy, and the sustaining power of human connection to heal.

**Michael's Epic Road Back from a Catastrophic Brain Injury**

It was a beautiful spring day in May 2006 when Michael Coss's life took an unimaginable turn.[4] The father of twin children was driving his family to Kelowna, British Columbia, for a work event, basking in the sunshine. In a still-unexplained incident, Michael suddenly lost control of his vehicle, which flipped violently end-over-end before coming to rest twisted and unrecognizable on the side of the road.

When the dust settled, a scene of miracles emerged - his wife escaped with just a broken wrist and their twin children with minor injuries. But Michael himself was unresponsive in the wreckage, having suffered a near-fatal traumatic brain injury that would leave him comatose for over six agonizing months. Doctors delivered a prognosis that would shake the family's core. If Michael ever regained consciousness at all, they cautioned, he would likely never walk, eat solid food, or utter a word again. He faced a life sentence of complete disability confined to a long-

---

4. https://www.youtube.com/watch?si=BH0Fx7fe33j-Lvzj&v=JWvKd8yEBWc&feature=youtu.be

term care facility - a dim future for a man who had once beamed with vitality.

But the once-doting husband and father still had a fight left in him. With little hope to go on, his family began researching alternative treatments and discovered hyperbaric oxygen therapy. After just three sessions in a hyperbaric chamber, Michael's eyes re-opened on Christmas Eve 2006, ending his half-year trapped in silent darkness.

His reawakening marked the start of an even more daunting new journey. When Michael first broke through to consciousness, the full extent of his impairments became clear - he could barely move his thumb and was unable to speak or swallow food. But he had been granted a second chance at life and was determined to make the most of it. With painstaking effort over the next two years, Michael relearned how to talk, chew, and perform basic motor functions like grasping objects. His family and medical team celebrated each modest milestone as a breakthrough in his incredible recovery.

Just nine months after emerging from his coma, despite still requiring a wheelchair and being unable to feed himself, Michael felt compelled to give back to others still struggling as he was. In an act that stunned even his own family, he used his limited mobility to launch a fundraising campaign for brain injury research with the Rick Hansen Foundation[5] - and raised an unprecedented $22,000 to set a new fundraising record.

Michael's resilience has inspired millions. In 2009, he created the Michael Coss Brain Injury Foundation to fund treatments like the hyperbaric therapy that saved his own life. He has mastered walking again and competed in the Vancouver Sun Run. His autobiography, *The Courage to Come Back*,[6] has uplifted fellow survivors globally.

While Michael's path has included serious challenges like a

---

5. https://www.rickhansen.com/
6. My Book

divorce in 2010, his perspective remains unshakable: "All things are possible when you believe." Having gone from virtually no chance of regaining speech, mobility, or independence to achieving milestones doctors thought impossible, Michael is living proof that the human spirit cannot be extinguished, and that hope is more powerful than any prognosis.

## Molly's Unstoppable Resilience: From Coma to Cap and Gown

It was supposed to be just a quick weekend trip home from Auburn University for twenty-year-old Molly Welch.[7] The ambitious journalism major had landed her dream job at the school newspaper and couldn't wait to share the exciting news with a friend. She grabbed her tape recorder on the way out, ready to capture some notes and interviews.

Molly never imagined that the same tape recorder would also capture the horrific sounds of her life shattering. While fiddling with the device, she took her eyes off the road for a split second. In that fateful moment of distraction, Molly's car veered across the median, slamming head-on into an oncoming pickup truck. The impact was catastrophic, leaving Molly with a diffuse axonal brain injury - an injury caused by the brain sheering and ripping from the sheer force of the collision. She lapsed into a coma for weeks, barely clinging to life, with minimal signs of consciousness for several agonizing months.

When Molly's parents raced to her bedside, the prognosis from doctors was devastating - she had just a 50% chance of surviving the night. And if she somehow pulled through, there was an equally grim outlook that she may never walk again. Against those formidable odds, Molly demonstrated her unstoppable will and determination from the start. As she gradually regained consciousness, the true test of her resilience began -

---

7. https://www.youtube.com/watch?v=pe64gyLjrBs

relearning the most basic tasks like brushing her teeth, talking, and putting one foot in front of the other.

Her recovery was a gruelingly slow process of reclaiming each stripped ability through intensive physical, occupational, and speech therapy. But Molly embraced every hard-fought achievement, taking each small, repetitive step with stoic resolve and a trademark bright smile.

One overriding goal powered Molly's recovery through it all - earning her Auburn journalism degree and walking across that stage at graduation, diploma in hand. "Nothing was going to stop that. I mean, nothing," her mother recalled. Molly's unbreakable spirit transformed the once-devastating prognosis into an inspiring reality.

In the years since defying death on that highway, Molly has channeled her lived experience into a mission of giving back and helping fellow brain injury survivors heal. She has volunteered countless hours at the renowned Atlanta-based Shepherd Center,[8] providing personalized peer support and living proof that a better life can blossom from unimaginable trauma.

Molly's warm presence, eternal optimism, and unapologetic zest for life have made her a *de facto* ambassador for what's possible after brain injury. Fellow survivors and their families can't help but be uplifted in her presence as a shining example that no diagnosis can define one's future. Whether she's regaling staff with her dry wit at Shepherd's welcome desk, mentoring newly injured patients, or fearlessly reliving her story to raise distracted driving awareness, Molly brings resilience to life in the most authentic and empowering way possible - by living it every day to its fullest.

The experience had another unexpected and unintended benefit - for us all. Molly became a staunch advocate against distracted driving. She often speaks about her accident to raise awareness of the dangers, hoping to prevent others from experi-

---

8. https://www.shepherd.org/

similar tragedies. Her story is a poignant reminder that even a momentary distraction, such as texting or fumbling with a cell phone, can have life-altering consequences.

## Kelly's Journey: When a Daughter's Miracle Becomes a Mother's Mission

It began like any other seemingly routine day for Kelly Lang and her family.[9] She was driving her two young daughters to dance rehearsal, her minivan packed with Tupperware and small talk and laughter. Kelly's last memory was an ordinary one - pulling out of their driveway, ready to embark on a short 5-mile journey they had made hundreds of times before.

What happened next would rupture their lives into a before and an after.

Out of nowhere, a vehicle violently rear-ended Kelly's minivan at an intersection. The tremendous force pushed her van forty feet across three lanes of traffic before it came to a crumpled halt, suspended atop a guardrail.

Dazed from the impact, Kelly was jolted back to consciousness by the piercing screams of her five-year-old daughter: "Mommy, mommy, wake up!" As strangers rushed to extract them from the mangled van, Kelly knew with a mother's intuition that something was wrong with her three-year-old strapped into a car seat behind her. She cried out desperately to the gathering rescuers, "Save her!"

At the hospital, the unthinkable was confirmed - Kelly's three-year-old daughter had sustained a severe traumatic brain injury in the horrific crash. The delicate toddler brain had been bruised and battered, leaving her in a coma with an uncertain future. Doctors warned the anguished parents to brace for their little girl perhaps never waking up.

Kelly and her husband could do little but gather at their

---

9. https://www.biausa.org/brain-injury/community/personal-stories/kelly-lang

daughter's bedside, watching her lifeless body with a kaleidoscope of emotions - hope, fear, sadness, helplessness. They were instructed not to touch or hold her, only to speak softly so as not to disrupt any signs of consciousness trying to break through. Then, after an agonizing nine-day vigil, their daughter's eyes fluttered open, slowly rejoining the living. While a huge initial victory, the family had only begun their arduous journey through the unpredictable recovery process from pediatric brain trauma. They took solace in the words of a pediatric neurologist who called their three-year-old daughter "the Miracle Child."

Even as their daughter made progress in an inpatient rehab program, Kelly began noticing unshakable symptoms in herself, too - exhaustion, inability to comprehend reading materials, and a short fuse with complex tasks like balancing her checkbook. When neuropsychologists confirmed Kelly had also sustained a brain injury in the crash, a new well of anguish opened. How could she be a capable caregiver when she, too, was suffering the debilitating fallout of a brain trauma?

Yet an unexpected upside to their parallel experiences emerged - Kelly understood her daughter's struggles in a uniquely insightful way as they were navigating many of the same unseen issues, like aphasia, i.e., a sudden inability to communicate. When her daughter encountered word-finding roadblocks, Kelly knew providing patient silence was better than jumping in with corrections.

Those small bonds of connection, born from their shared lives being upended by brain injury, gave both mother and daughter the fortitude and empathy to continue persevering day by day. In the decade-plus since the life-altering van crash, the two have supported each other through an array of deficits, therapies, and triumphs. They have found replenishing inspiration to celebrate the small joys that often get taken for granted - a flower blooming, a good book, and laughing with friends over coffee.

More importantly, Kelly has undergone her transformation from survivor to outspoken advocate on a mission to help other brain injury families move forward. She shares their story through public speeches to educate emergency responders, healthcare professionals, and others about the upheaval that brain injury creates in all aspects of life. Indeed, her work evolved into a broader advocacy for brain injury survivors, caregivers, and families. Kelly and her husband, Michael, recently co-wrote the book *The Miracle Child: Traumatic Brain Injury and Me*,[10] chronicling their family's journey and offering hope to others who have experienced similar life-altering events.

At the time of the accident, Michael had been recently laid off, and the family was saddled with a mortgage on a brand-new house. Although there were many hardships over the ensuing fifteen years, the tragedy brought the family closer together, with each spouse committed to helping the other. Ultimately, Kelly's journey led her to an invaluable piece of wisdom about coping with a life re-routed by unexpected trauma:

"We must let go of the life we had planned so as to accept the one that is waiting for us."

**Strategies for Adapting to Life with TBI**

While each traumatic brain injury recovery journey is unique, the powerful stories highlighted in this chapter demonstrate that regaining fulfillment after brain trauma is possible with the right mindset, support, and strategies in place. From Michael Coss's unprecedented determination to Dylan's defiance of a grim prognosis to Molly Welch's resilience in reclaiming her independence step-by-step, these survivors model an array of effective approaches for reconstructing one's life and sense of identity post-injury.

---

10. My Book

**Adopt a "Survivor" Mentality.** A commonality across their narratives is the refusal to be constrained by their diagnosis or doctors' predictions. Time and again, we see these individuals actively fight against labels like "permanently disabled" through sheer grit and perseverance. Michael Coss epitomized this mentality in his declaration, "All things are possible when you believe," after achieving milestones like walking and talking that medical experts had deemed improbable. Maintaining an "I'll show them" mindset and goalposts to work towards actively can be an immensely motivating force on the long road of rehabilitation.

**Find Your "Why."** Traumatic brain injuries invariably derail one's life plan in a tumultuous way. Having driving motivators or "whys" to recover for can make accessibility challenges more surmountable. For Molly Welch, the vision of walking across the stage at her college graduation bestowed her with profound resilience through the highs and lows of rehab. Dylan's steely determination was fueled by the dream of one day strolling hand-in-hand through parks with his children again. Identifying these temporal, tangible "whys" can give needed boosts on difficult days.

### Celebrate Every Incremental Victory

Recovering from a severe TBI is a slow, arduous journey of relearning basic skills most take for granted - speaking, reading, brushing one's teeth, etc. Celebrating and savoring each incremental progress point, no matter how small, is crucial for maintaining motivation. When Michael Coss's family initially doubted his ability to raise $22,000 for charity from a care facility, he defied their expectations through relentless determination to type with just his thumb—recognizing that achievement as a milestone worth commemorating paid psychological dividends for taking on new challenges.

**Accept It Will Be a Marathon, Not a Sprint.** The common view for brain injury rehabilitation has shifted from prescribing full rest to promoting active rehabilitation and a graded return to normal routines as tolerated. Dylan was still making incredible strides a full year after his traumatic accident. Molly's recovery allowed her to build inspiring stamina - progressing from relearning to brush her teeth to completing thousands of hours of peer mentoring at Shepherd years later. Adopting a mindset that healing will be an incremental, ongoing process rather than an event with a finite finish line can make the arduous feel more accessible.

**Embrace Compensatory Strategies.** When struggling with cognitive issues like short-term memory problems or aphasia, leaning on tools like journals, notes, and organizational systems can be helpful. Ann Boriskie improvised "workarounds," such as leaving herself reminder notes. Molly channeled her natural gregariousness into working guest services roles that were well-suited to her outgoing personality. Identifying and accepting your new normal and then exploring modifications can help overcome accessibility hurdles.

The unifying refrain from survivors like Michael, Molly, Ann, Kelly, and Dylan is that brain injury recoveries are formidable battles but winnable ones with the proper blend of persistence, creativity, self-compassion, and meaningful "whys." Equally crucial, however, is cultivating a network of support sources to help light the way.

. . .

**Organizations and Help Are Available.** The power of peer connections and support groups cannot be overstated. As Ann Boriskie's Brain Injury Peer Visitor Association model demonstrates, having the ability to learn from and lean on others who have navigated similar trauma can make the dense fog of a brain injury feel less isolating. Simply bonding with people who genuinely say, "I know what you're going through," provides an incomparable sense of community.

On a practical level, getting plugged into local brain injury advocacy groups and nonprofits helps access wide-ranging resources and accelerate education. From networking with experts on legal rights and disability benefits to getting referrals for specialized therapists and treatment programs, these organizations empower survivors and caregivers to become their own best advocates.

Underscoring all these efforts is the fundamental need for accurate, science-backed information and awareness around brain injury's complexities and misconceptions. Trusted educational sources such as the Centers for Disease Control's HEADS UP campaign[11] equip people with facts over fiction about conditions like concussions. Increasingly, preventive efforts and guidelines are being adopted in arenas from youth sports to the military to identify brain injuries earlier and mitigate impacts through prompt treatment.

No growth journey is easy, but embracing an open mindset towards exploring compensatory strategies, redefining benchmarks of success, and building a robust local and online support system can light an achievable pathway forward for individuals and families impacted by brain trauma. The uplifting examples set by survivors like those highlighted in this chapter prove that

---

11. https://www.cdc.gov/headsup/index.html

with reserves of hope, resilience, and community, a fulfilling life after brain injury is possible.

# 12

# FINDING HOPE, EMPOWERMENT, AND RESOURCES AFTER TBI

### The Unstoppable Spirit of Karla Dougan

In the face of a life-altering event like a traumatic brain injury (TBI), it can be challenging to find hope and purpose. However, as we've seen throughout this book, countless TBI survivors have demonstrated remarkable resilience and have gone on to make a positive impact in their communities. One such inspiring example is the story of Karla Dougan, a University of Georgia student who suffered a severe TBI in a car accident.[1]

Despite the overwhelming obstacles she faced, including multiple surgeries, intensive rehabilitation, and the need to use a wheelchair, Karla refused to let her injury define her. With unwavering determination, she pursued her dreams of attending college and became one of the few students in a wheelchair to rush a sorority. Her father, Scott Dougan, a cellular biology professor at UGA, praised the sororities for their inclusivity and willingness to accommodate Karla's needs.

---

1. https://www.ajc.com/blog/get-schooled/uga-changes-honor-rules-include-more-students-with-disabilities/ZRit22ycylNzkqviGbdefJ/

Karla's resilience and positive outlook led her to become an advocate for TBI awareness. She created a powerful video for the Governor's Office of Highway Safety, sharing her story and warning others about the dangers of distracted driving. Her message resonated with viewers, emphasizing the importance of responsible driving habits and the life-altering consequences of a single moment of inattention behind the wheel.

Stories like Karla's remind us that even in the darkest of times, there is hope for recovery and the opportunity to make a difference. Throughout my years as an attorney, I have had the privilege of witnessing the incredible strength and resolve of clients and families affected by injuries like TBIs. Their experiences helped shape my career–advocating for their rights and helping them on their road to recovery.

In this final chapter, I want to explore the importance of finding hope and purpose after a TBI, celebrate the progress made in TBI awareness and treatment, and discuss the role of advocacy in driving change. I will also provide resources for empowerment and support, ensuring that TBI survivors and their families have access to the tools they need to thrive in the face of adversity.

**The Importance of Finding Hope and Purpose After a TBI**

Sustaining a traumatic brain injury can be an overwhelming experience, leading to feelings of despair, isolation, and a loss of identity. However, as noted in the stories of TBI survivors throughout this book, finding hope and purpose in the aftermath of a TBI is necessary for both emotional well-being and the recovery process. When survivors and their families focus on setting goals, celebrating small victories, and finding meaning in their experiences, they can cultivate a sense of resilience and empowerment.

One way to find purpose is by connecting with others who have undergone similar challenges. Support groups, both in-person and online, provide a platform for survivors and caregivers to share their stories, offer encouragement, and exchange valuable resources. Engaging with these communities can help foster a sense of belonging and remind individuals that they are not alone in their struggles.

Another path to finding meaning is through advocacy and raising awareness about TBI. By sharing their experiences and educating others about the impact of brain injuries, survivors can help break down stigmas and promote understanding. Many survivors we've met in this book have helped themselves and others through public speaking, writing, or participating in events hosted by brain injury organizations.

Finding hope and purpose after a TBI is a deeply personal journey that may look different for each individual. In your time of trial, you will discover your pillars of strength. Some may find solace in their faith, while others may discover new passions or creative outlets. The key is to remain open to possibilities and to lean on the support of loved ones and professionals who can help guide the way.

## Celebrating the Progress in TBI Awareness and Treatment

Significant progress has been made in TBI awareness and treatment in recent years. These advancements offer hope to survivors and their families as they demonstrate a growing understanding of the complexities of brain injuries and a commitment to improving outcomes. We still have a long way to go in raising public awareness and improving TBI treatment, but I'd like to mention a few of the positive developments I've noticed:

**Increased Public Awareness and Understanding of TBI.** One notable area of progress is the increased public awareness and understanding of TBIs. High-profile cases involving athletes, military personnel, and celebrities have helped bring attention to the serious nature of brain injuries and the need for prevention and proper treatment. This heightened awareness has led to more open discussions about TBIs, reducing the stigma surrounding the injuries and encouraging more people to seek help.

**Advancements in Medical Research and Rehabilitation Techniques.** The scientific community has made significant strides in understanding the mechanisms of TBIs and developing innovative treatment approaches. Researchers are exploring new diagnostic tools, such as advanced neuroimaging techniques, that can detect subtle changes in brain function and guide personalized treatment plans. Additionally, there have been advancements in rehabilitation techniques, including virtual reality therapy, cognitive training programs, and non-invasive brain stimulation methods, which aim to enhance the brain's natural healing processes.

**Policy Changes that Protect TBI Survivors.** Progress has also been made in implementing policy changes that protect TBI survivors. One notable example is the development of return-to-play guidelines for athletes. These guidelines, adopted by many sports organizations, provide a structured protocol for assessing and managing concussions, ensuring that athletes do not return to play prematurely and risk further injury. Similar policies have been implemented in the military and various occupational settings to promote the safety and well-being of individuals at risk for a TBI.

One notable example of such policy changes is the implementation of "Return to Play" laws for youth sports in many states.[2] These laws require coaches, parents, and athletes to be

---

2. https://www.cdc.gov/headsup/policy/index.html

educated about concussion recognition and management and establish clear protocols for removing athletes from play when a concussion is suspected. Such policies help protect young athletes from the risks of repeated brain injuries and ensure that they receive appropriate medical care before returning to sports.

**Shared Stories Raise Awareness.** One of the most effective ways TBI survivors and their families can contribute to advocacy is by sharing their personal experiences. By speaking out about the challenges they face, the triumphs they achieve, and the gaps in the current system, they can put a human face on the issue of TBIs and inspire others to act. I have noticed an ever-increasing number of public forums, including social media, blogs, podcasts, and local news outlets. These shared stories connect survivors and families with others who have undergone similar experiences, creating a sense of community and support.

**TBI Research Offers New Resources for Survivors.** Organizations such as the Brain Injury Association of America,[3] the Concussion Legacy Foundation,[4] and the TBI Model Systems[5] advocate for survivors and offer pathways to new treatments. While much work is still needed in TBI care and research, celebrating these milestones helps us see how far we've come. They serve as a reminder that the tireless efforts of advocates, researchers, and healthcare professionals are making a difference in the lives of TBI survivors and their families. As we look to the future, we can take solace in knowing that advancements will continue, bringing us closer to a world where every TBI survivor can access the best possible care and support.

---

3. https://www.biausa.org/
4. https://concussionfoundation.org/
5. https://msktc.org/about-model-systems/TBI

### Resources for Empowerment and Support

Navigating life after a TBI can be overwhelming, but there are numerous resources available to help survivors and their families feel empowered and supported. These resources can provide valuable information, emotional support, and practical guidance as individuals work towards recovery and adaptation.

**Brain Injury Associations and Support Groups.** One of the most valuable resources for TBI survivors and their families are brain injury associations and support groups. These organizations, which operate at the national, state, and local levels, offer various services, including educational materials, referrals to healthcare providers, and peer support programs. Connecting with these organizations can help individuals feel less alone and more equipped to handle life's challenges after TBI.

**Online Communities and Forums for TBI Survivors and Caregivers.** In addition to in-person support groups, there are many online communities and forums designed explicitly for TBI survivors and caregivers. These digital spaces allow individuals to connect with others who understand their experiences, share advice and coping strategies, and provide emotional support. Some popular online resources include the Brain Injury Peer Visitor Association,[6] the Brain Injury Association of America,[7] and the Institute on Aging.[8]

---

6. https://braininjurypeervisitor.org/
7. https://www.biausa.org/
8. https://www.ioaging.org/caregiving/traumatic-brain-injury-support-groups-online-and-near-me-in-the-bay-area/

**Counseling and Therapy Services to Aid in Emotional Recovery.** The emotional impact of a TBI can be just as significant as the physical and cognitive effects. Many survivors and their families benefit from counseling and therapy services to support emotional recovery. These services can help individuals process the grief, anxiety, and depression that often accompany a TBI, as well as develop coping strategies and communication skills. Some specialized therapy options include cognitive-behavioral therapy, family therapy, and neuropsychological counseling.

In addition to these resources, there are comprehensive guides and knowledge centers available to help TBI survivors and their families better understand the complexities of brain injury recovery. The Brain Injury Association of America offers a detailed "Brain Injury Guide and Resources" on their website,[9] covering topics ranging from understanding TBI to finding legal and financial support. Another valuable resource is the "TBI Model Systems Knowledge Translation Center,"[10] which provides evidence-based information and resources on TBI rehabilitation and recovery, including factsheets, videos, and research updates.

By taking advantage of these resources and support systems, TBI survivors and their families can find strength and hope in the face of hardship. Remember, no one should take the journey of TBI recovery alone. A vast network of professionals, organizations, and fellow survivors is ready to offer guidance and support at every step.

---

9. https://www.biausa.org/wp-content/uploads/Guide-for-Families-and-Caregivers.pdf
10. https://msktc.org/tbi/factsheets/understanding-traumatic-brain-injury

*The Importance of Hope and Resilience in the Face of TBI*

Throughout this book, we have explored the many facets of life after a traumatic brain injury, from the initial shock of diagnosis to the long road to recovery and adaptation. We have discussed the legal, medical, and emotional challenges that survivors and their families face and the resources and support systems available to help them navigate this difficult journey.

At the heart of the long struggle ahead are two words I want all TBI survivors and their families to always carry with them: hope and resilience. They strengthened me when I grappled with a brain tumor and years of post-operative complications – and they will strengthen you.

Hope is the driving force that propels survivors and their loved ones forward, even in the darkest of times. It is the belief that recovery is possible, that a meaningful life can be rebuilt, and that the future holds promise.

Resilience, on the other hand, is the adaptability that allows individuals to persevere in the face of adversity, to solve problems creatively, and to grow and learn from their experiences.

Cultivating hope and resilience requires a conscious effort to focus on the positive, to celebrate small victories, and to surround oneself with supportive and uplifting influences. It also means being kind and patient with oneself, acknowledging that setbacks and difficult days are a normal part of the journey and not a reflection of personal failure.

By embracing hope and resilience, TBI survivors and their families can tap into a powerful source of stability and motivation and find the courage to keep pushing forward, even when the path ahead seems daunting.

# 13

# EPILOGUE: TAKE THE NEXT STEPS

**How to Protect Your Rights and Secure Your Future**

Thanks to survivors, advocates, healthcare professionals, and researchers, we have seen significant advancements in TBI awareness, research, and treatment in recent years. Public understanding of TBI has grown, leading to more open conversations and a reduction in the stigma surrounding brain injuries. Medical research has yielded new insights into the mechanisms of TBI and the most effective strategies for promoting recovery. Rehabilitation techniques have become more sophisticated and personalized, giving survivors access to cutting-edge therapies and support services.

However, despite the importance of prompt medical care and the advancements in awareness and treatments, nearly half of all TBIs go undiagnosed. This is because TBIs are often "closed" injuries, meaning that the damage is not visible from the outside of the skull. Additionally, the changes in a person's behavior and abilities after a TBI may not be immediately obvious to the individual or their loved ones.

Many TBI survivors and their families continue to face

barriers in accessing quality care, navigating complex legal and insurance systems, and finding the support they need to thrive. It is common to feel overwhelmed, confused, and unsure about the next steps. It is important to remember that you are not alone; tens of thousands of people face the challenges of TBI every year, and many of them are unsure where to seek help.

To protect your legal rights and secure your future, it is essential to take action. By understanding your legal options and seeking the guidance of a TBI attorney, you can take control of your situation and work towards the best possible outcome for you and your family.

**Understanding Your Legal Rights**

If you or your loved one has suffered a traumatic brain injury (TBI) because of the negligent action of others, you may be entitled to compensation for your medical expenses, lost wages, pain and suffering, and other damages, depending on the circumstances surrounding your injury.

However, navigating the complex legal system can be overwhelming, especially when you are already coping with the physical and emotional challenges that come with a TBI. This is why it is crucial to seek the guidance of a skilled TBI attorney who has experience handling these unique cases and can guide you through the process.

A knowledgeable TBI attorney can provide invaluable assistance by:

1. Thoroughly investigating the cause of your injury and identifying all liable parties.
2. Gathering crucial evidence to support your claim, such as medical records and witness statements.
3. Accurately calculating the full extent of your damages, including future medical expenses and lost earning capacity.

4. Negotiating with insurance companies and other parties to secure a fair settlement on your behalf.
5. Representing you in court, if necessary, to fiercely advocate for your rights.

By working with an attorney who focuses on TBI cases, you can ensure that your interests are protected. Your attorney will be your advocate, understanding the challenges you face and working to help you secure the compensation you deserve. Don't face this difficult time alone; seek the help of a skilled TBI attorney to fight for the justice and support you need to move forward with your life.

Delay doesn't pay. Neglecting to pursue a valid TBI case can lead to significant financial hardships for you and your family. By taking prompt legal action, you can work with your attorney to gather essential evidence, document your injuries, and build a strong case while the details of the incident are still fresh in your mind and the minds of potential witnesses.

However, if some time has passed since your injury, don't assume that it's too late to seek legal guidance. Even if you've waited weeks, months, or longer, it's still worthwhile to consult with a TBI attorney to discuss your options. While certain legal deadlines may apply, an experienced attorney can help you understand your rights and determine the best course of action based on your unique circumstances. They can also help you navigate the complex legal and medical systems, ensuring that you receive the care and support you need to move forward with your life.

By pursuing a valid TBI case, you can secure essential compensation that covers your existing medical expenses, future unreimbursed costs, and the pain and suffering you have endured and may continue to face. Such compensation can also help replace lost income and provide the support that you and your loved ones need after a radically life-changing event.

Pursuing your TBI claim is not just about securing the financial resources you require; it is also about holding accountable those whose negligence or misconduct caused your injury. By taking legal action, you can help prevent similar incidents from happening to others in the future. Your case can serve as a powerful reminder that careless or reckless behavior has consequences and that those responsible must be held liable for the harm they have caused.

You have the opportunity to seek justice and protect your financial future. Your best course of action is to consult with a skilled TBI attorney who can guide you through the legal process and fight for the compensation and accountability you deserve.

**Hackard Law Focuses on TBI Cases**

Laws and cases are complex. When facing the challenges of a TBI, you should look for a law firm that understands the legal aspects of your case and the personal and emotional impact of your injury. At Hackard Law, we have a unique perspective on TBI cases, thanks to my personal journey, and many years of helping clients deal with injury cases.

I have firsthand knowledge of the struggles that TBI survivors face. My battle with a brain tumor and the subsequent challenges I encountered gave me a deep understanding of the physical, cognitive, and emotional toll that a brain injury can take. My firm and I are veterans and fierce advocates for the rights of our clients.

In addition to my personal experience, Hackard Law has a proven track record of success in handling TBI cases. Our team has represented many clients who have suffered brain injuries because of the actions of others. We have the knowledge, resources, and dedication to build strong cases and fight for the compensation our clients deserve.

At Hackard Law, we understand that taking legal action can be overwhelming, especially when dealing with the financial burden of medical expenses and lost income. That's why we work on a contingency basis, meaning you don't pay any upfront costs to hire us. We only get paid if we secure a settlement or verdict in your favor so you can focus on your recovery without worrying about the legal fees.

Here are just two of the many endorsements our clients have given us:

> "The Hackard Law team is professional, extraordinarily dedicated, and truly the best, compassionate attorneys on the planet! Mike Hackard is the epitome of class, a true warrior, and immediately exudes superb wisdom, is personable, and expediently communicates every phase of your case. There is unequivocally no other law firm of such high caliber." - David S.

> "Hackard Law went above and beyond to help me resolve a very difficult estate case. Although I am completely inexperienced when it comes to the legal system, Mike Hackard answered all my questions with clarity and respect, and he walked me through the whole process. I would definitely recommend Mike Hackard for legal counsel." - Denise W.

We are committed to our clients and dedicated to achieving the best possible outcomes in every case we handle. When you work with Hackard Law, you're not just hiring a lawyer; you're gaining a team of experienced, compassionate advocates who will stand by your side every step.

## It's Important to Act Quickly

If you or a loved one has suffered a TBI, it's important to act quickly to protect your legal rights. In California, the statute of limitations for most personal injury cases, including TBI cases, is two years from the date of the injury. You have this limited time to file a lawsuit and seek compensation for your damages.

While two years may seem like a long time, it's important to remember that building a strong TBI case takes time, time for documenting injuries and lost compensation, gathering evidence, and speaking with the relevant parties. The sooner you seek legal advice, the better your chances of securing a favorable outcome. Early legal intervention can help you:

- Preserve critical evidence, such as accident scene photos, witness statements, and medical records.
- Document the full extent of your injuries and their impact on your life.
- Identify and pursue all potential sources of compensation, such as insurance policies and liable parties.
- Avoid common mistakes that could harm your case, such as giving recorded statements to insurance adjusters or signing settlement offers without consulting an attorney.

If you wait too long to file a lawsuit, you may not be able to recover any compensation. Also, the longer you wait, the harder it may be to gather evidence and build a strong case. Witnesses may forget important details, evidence may be lost or destroyed, and the full impact of your injuries may become more difficult to prove.

Don't wait until it's too late. Don't let legal technicalities or other delays jeopardize your right to fair compensation. If you suspect that you or a loved one has suffered a TBI, contact an experienced attorney at Hackard Law as soon as possible to discuss your legal options.

## How to Schedule a Consultation with Hackard Law

We understand that taking the first step towards legal action can seem overwhelming. That's why we've made it easy for you to schedule a consultation with our expert TBI attorneys.

To get started, contact our office using one of the following methods:

- Call us at (916) 313-3030
- Email us at info@hackardlaw.com
- Fill out the online contact form on our website at https://www.hackardlaw.com

When you reach out, one of Hackard Law's friendly and knowledgeable staff members will gather some basic information about your case and schedule a convenient time for you to speak with one of our attorneys. We offer phone, video conference, or in-person consultations at our office in Mather, California, near Sacramento.

During your consultation, you'll be able to discuss your case with a knowledgeable TBI attorney who can answer your questions, explain your legal options, and help you decide the best path forward. We'll listen to your story with compassion and respect and provide you with honest and straightforward advice about your case.

Your consultation will be completely confidential and comes with no obligation to hire our firm. We're here to help you make informed decisions about your legal rights and give you the support and guidance you need during this challenging time.

**Don't Suffer in Silence**

The physical, emotional, and financial consequences of a TBI can be overwhelming, but you don't have to face them alone. At Hackard Law, we understand the challenges you're facing, and we're here to help.

Every voice matters in the fight to improve the lives of those affected by TBI, and I encourage all readers to consider how they can contribute to this vital cause. Whether volunteering, donating, or simply spreading awareness, every action brings us closer to a world where all TBI survivors have access to the care, support, and opportunities they deserve.

To all the TBI survivors and their loved ones reading this book, never underestimate your resilience or the power of the support systems around you. Keep holding onto hope, even in the most difficult moments, and know that you are not alone.

Let us continue to raise awareness, advocate for change, and support one another. Let us move forward with determination, unity, and an unwavering commitment to building a better tomorrow for all those affected by traumatic brain injury.

# 14

# A FEW IMPORTANT TBI MEDICAL RESOURCES IN CALIFORNIA

**California Medical Centers Specializing in TBI and mTBI Treatment and Research**

These California Medical Centers are known for their expertise in treating both traumatic brain injury (TBI) and mild traumatic brain injury (mTBI). They also do research, offer specialized care, use advanced diagnostic tools, and employ multidisciplinary approaches to patient care and research.

**UCLA Brain Injury Research Center (BIRC), Los Angeles**

Conducts research and provides clinical care for mTBI patients. Part of the UCLA Department of Neurosurgery

Address: 300 Stein Plaza, Suite 536, Los Angeles, CA 90095
Phone: (310) 206-3207
Email: info@birc.ucla.edu
Website: https://birc.ucla.edu/

## UCSF Memory and Aging Center, San Francisco

Specializes in the diagnosis and treatment of neurological disorders, including mTBI.
Offers a multidisciplinary approach to patient care and research.

Address: 675 Nelson Rising Lane, Suite 190
San Francisco, CA 94158
Phone: (415) 353-2057
Email: mac@memory.ucsf.edu
Website: https://memory.ucsf.edu/

## Scripps Memorial Hospital, La Jolla

Houses the Scripps Concussion Program, which provides comprehensive care for mTBI patients.
Utilizes advanced diagnostic tools and individualized treatment plans.

Address: 9888 Genesee Ave, La Jolla, CA 92037
Phone: (858) 626-4123 (Scripps Concussion Program)
Website: https://www.scripps.org/services/brain-and-spine/concussion-program

## Cedars-Sinai Medical Center, Los Angeles

Features a dedicated Neurology and Neurosurgery Department
Provides expert care for mTBI patients and conducts research on brain injuries.

Address: 127 S. San Vicente Blvd., Suite A6600, Los Angeles, CA 90048
Phone: (310) 423-7420 (Neurology Department)

Website: https://www.cedars-sinai.org/programs/neurology-neurosurgery.html

### Stanford Concussion and Brain Performance Center, Stanford

Offers comprehensive care for mTBI patients, from diagnosis to rehabilitation.
Conducts research to improve the understanding and treatment of concussions.

Address: 341 Galvez Street, Stanford, CA 94305
Phone: (650) 725-5106
Email: brainperformance@stanford.edu
Website: https://med.stanford.edu/cbpc.html

### UC Davis Health, Sacramento

Houses the UC Davis Center for Neuroscience, which includes a Neurotrauma Research Group
Provides clinical care for mTBI patients and conducts research on brain injuries.

Address: 4860 Y Street, Suite 3700, Sacramento, CA 95817
Phone: (916) 734-5441 (Neurology Clinic)
Website: https://health.ucdavis.edu/neurology/

### Kerlan-Jobe Center for Sports Neurology, Los Angeles

Specializes in the diagnosis and treatment of sports-related concussions and mTBI.
Utilizes a multidisciplinary approach to patient care, including neurology, neuropsychology, and physical therapy.

Address: 6801 Park Terrace Drive, Suite 400, Los Angeles, CA 90045
Phone: (310) 665-7145
Email: info@kerlanjobe.org
Website: https://www.kerlanjobe.org/sports-neurology/

**Resources for Veterans**

The U.S. Department of Veterans Affairs (VA) recognizes TBI and mTBI as significant concerns for veterans, particularly those who have served in combat zones.[1] The VA provides comprehensive information, resources, and support for veterans with mTBI, including a definition of mTBI, acknowledgment of its wide-ranging symptoms, emphasis on timely and accurate diagnosis, and various treatment options.

The VA has established the Polytrauma/TBI System of Care, a comprehensive program that provides specialized care and support for veterans with mTBI and other complex injuries through a network of specialized centers, multidisciplinary teams, and resources.

Here are some key points from the VA regarding mTBI:

**Definition:** The VA defines mTBI as a traumatically induced structural injury and/or physiological disruption of brain function as a result of an external force, indicated by at least one of the following: loss of consciousness, loss of memory for events immediately before or after the injury, alteration in mental state at the time of the injury, or focal neurological deficits.

---

1. https://www.mentalhealth.va.gov/tbi/index.asp

. . .

**Symptoms:** The VA acknowledges that mTBI can cause a wide range of physical, cognitive, emotional, and behavioral symptoms, such as headaches, dizziness, memory problems, difficulty concentrating, irritability, and sleep disturbances.

**Diagnosis:** The VA emphasizes the importance of timely and accurate diagnosis of mTBI. Diagnosis may involve neurological examinations, cognitive assessments, imaging tests, and other specialized evaluations.

**Treatment:** The VA provides a variety of treatment options for veterans with mTBI, including medication management, rehabilitation services (e.g., physical therapy, occupational therapy, speech-language therapy), cognitive rehabilitation, and psychological support.

**Long-term effects:** The VA recognizes that some veterans may experience persistent symptoms or develop long-term complications following mTBI, such as post-concussive syndrome, chronic pain, or mental health disorders like post-traumatic stress disorder (PTSD) or depression.

**Research:** The VA conducts and supports extensive research on mTBI to better understand its effects on veterans, improve diagnostic methods, and develop new treatment strategies.

**Benefits:** Veterans with service-connected mTBI may be eligible for various VA benefits, including disability compensation, healthcare services, and vocational rehabilitation.

The VA has established a comprehensive program called the Polytrauma/TBI System of Care to provide specialized care and support for veterans with mTBI and other complex injuries. This system includes a network of specialized centers, multidisciplinary teams, and resources to address the unique needs of veterans with mTBI.

# 15

# GLOSSARY OF TERMS

**Adynamia:** Apathy, loss of drive. The individual is no longer dynamic or energetic and may appear to lack motivation. Responses to others or to situations are dull, flat. There is slowed mental functioning, a marked decrease in ideas, activity is rarely self-initiated.

**Aggression:** Hostile or violent behavior intended to cause harm, dominate, or intimidate others, either physically or verbally.

**Agitation:** A state of excessive restlessness, irritability, and anxiety, often accompanied by repetitive or purposeless movements.

**Altered Consciousness:** Associated with a TBI, changes in awareness, responsiveness, and cognitive function following a traumatic brain injury, which can range from mild confusion and disorientation to more severe states like stupor, coma, or vegetative state.

**Alteration in mental state:** A change in a person's mental status or awareness at the time of the injury, which may include confusion, disorientation, or feeling dazed.

**Amnesia:** Memory loss surrounding the event of the injury.

**Anhedonia:** The diminished or complete loss of the capacity to experience pleasure or enjoyment from activities or stimuli that an individual previously found rewarding, often associated with depression and other mental health disorders.

**Anterograde amnesia:** Difficulty forming new memories after the injury.

**Anxiety:** Excessive worry or fear.

**Apathy:** A lack of interest, motivation, or concern for activities, events, or relationships that were previously engaging, often accompanied by emotional flatness and reduced goal-directed behavior.

**Aphasia:** The inability to comprehend and/or to express language. This may include written or spoken words, ideas, or sign language. It may be a partial or complete impairment.

**Aplastic Anemia:** A rare condition in which the body fails to produce enough new blood cells, which can be a severe adverse reaction to certain medications.

**Apraxia:** The inability to perform a well-known, purposeful action in spite of having normal mobility, attention, and comprehension.

**Attention deficits:** Difficulties in maintaining focus, concentration, and mental engagement on a specific task or stimulus for an appropriate duration, often characterized by distractibility, forgetfulness, and disorganization, which can impact various aspects of daily life and learning.

**Autonomic dysfunction:** Disturbances in functions like heart rate, blood pressure, or temperature regulation.

**Balance Error Scoring System (BESS):** A simple, cost-effective tool for assessing static postural stability, consisting of three stances performed on two different surfaces.

**Balance problems:** Difficulty maintaining balance or coordinating movements.

**Behavioral changes:** Alterations in a person's typical behavior patterns.

**Behavioral Manifestations:** Three common organic behaviors associated with head injury are adynamia, disinhibition, and flooding. These are the result of injury to the frontal lobes of the brain as well as to the temporal lobes and the hypothalamus.

**Benign Brain Tumor:** A non-cancerous growth in the brain that, while not malignant, can still cause symptoms and require treatment.

**Biomarkers:** Measurable indicators of biological processes, pathogenic processes, or pharmacologic responses to therapeutic interventions, which can be used to diagnose, monitor, or predict the presence, severity, or progression of a disease or the effectiveness of a treatment.

**Blood Biomarkers:** Potential markers in the blood that researchers are investigating for diagnosing mTBI, such as S100B, GFAP, NSE, and tau protein.

**Brain Stem:** That part of the brain which connects the spinal cord with the hemispheres of the brain. The brain stem also regulates consciousness, heart rate, breathing, eye movements, and swallowing.

**Cervical strain:** A soft tissue injury to the muscles, tendons, or ligaments of the neck, often caused by sudden or prolonged awkward movements, leading to pain, stiffness, and reduced range of motion in the neck and upper back.

**Closed Head Injury (CHI):** Damage to the brain that is not accompanied by a fractured skull or a penetrating injury (such as a bullet that pierces the skull). CHI usually causes diffuse damage to the brain and affects many areas of function.

**Cognitive assessments:** Tests or evaluations that measure various aspects of cognitive function, such as memory, attention, concentration, and problem-solving skills.

**Cognitive impairment:** A term that describes a wide range of conditions that affect a person's ability to think, remember, reason, concentrate, and perform daily activities. It can range from mild to severe and may be caused by various factors, such as aging, brain injury, mental health disorders, or neurological diseases. Symptoms may include memory loss, confusion, difficulty communicating, and changes in behavior or personality.

**Cognitive rehabilitation:** A type of therapy that aims to improve or restore cognitive functions affected by mTBI, such as memory, attention, and executive functioning.

**Cognitive Testing:** Assessments used to evaluate cognitive function following a suspected mTBI, such as the Standardized Assessment of Concussion (SAC) and the Immediate Post-Concussion Assessment and Cognitive Testing (ImPACT).

**Coma:** A state of profound unconsciousness in which a person cannot be awakened, fails to respond normally to pain, light, or sound, and does not initiate voluntary actions. It is caused by severe brain injury or illness and can last from several days to weeks, months, or even years.

**Computed Tomography (CT) Scan:** An imaging test that uses X-rays to create detailed images of the brain, helping to identify fractures, bleeding, or other structural damage.

**Concussion:** A traumatic brain injury caused by a blow, bump, or jolt to the head, leading to temporary impairment of brain function, which may include symptoms such as headache, confusion, dizziness, memory loss, and difficulty concentrating.

**Confusion:** A state of being bewildered or unclear in one's thinking.

**Consequences of a TBI:** Can include physical, cognitive, emotional, and behavioral changes, such as headaches, memory loss, difficulty concentrating, mood swings, and impaired motor function, which may be temporary or permanent, depending on the severity of the injury.

**Depression:** Persistent feelings of sadness, hopelessness, or loss of interest in activities.

**Diffuse axonal injury (DAI):** A severe traumatic brain injury resulting from rapid acceleration-deceleration forces, causing widespread damage to axons (nerve fibers) throughout the brain, leading to cognitive impairments, loss of consciousness, and potentially prolonged coma or vegetative state.

**Disability compensation:** A monthly monetary benefit paid to veterans with service-connected disabilities, including mTBI.

**Disinhibition:** Loss of restraint in social or emotional behavior; a decrease in the ability to control impulsive behavior.

**Disorientation:** A state of mental confusion characterized by a lack of awareness or understanding of one's surroundings, time, personal identity, or situation, often resulting from factors such as illness, injury, or intoxication, and leading to feelings of bewilderment or perplexity.

**Dizziness:** A feeling of lightheadedness, unsteadiness, or loss of balance.

**Drowsiness:** A state of feeling abnormally sleepy or ready to fall asleep.

**Emotional lability:** Rapid and unpredictable changes in mood. Key characteristics of emotional lability include:
Rapid mood swings: Individuals can quickly switch from one emotional state to another, such as from happiness to sadness or from calmness to anger.
Unpredictable changes: The mood shifts often occur without warning or apparent trigger, making it difficult for the individual and others to anticipate or understand the emotional changes.
Intensity: The emotions experienced during these mood swings can be intense and may seem exaggerated compared to the situation at hand.
Difficulty regulating emotions: People with emotional lability may struggle to control or modulate their emotional responses, leading to impulsive behaviors or reactions.
Emotional lability can be a symptom of various neurological conditions, such as traumatic brain injury, stroke, or certain neurodegenerative diseases like Alzheimer's or Parkinson's disease. It can also be associated with mental health disorders, including borderline personality disorder, bipolar disorder, and post-traumatic stress disorder (PTSD).

Treatment for emotional lability typically involves a combination of medication, psychotherapy, and coping strategies to help individuals manage their emotions and improve their overall quality of life.

**Executive dysfunction:** Difficulties with planning, organizing, and problem-solving.

**Executive Function:** The ability to organize thoughts and work, to create plans and successfully execute them, to manage the administrative functions of one's life.

**Fatigue:** Extreme tiredness and lack of energy.

**Flooding:** Overwhelmed by, or awash in, one's emotions. This can take place even though the flooded individual does not appear upset or distraught or even consciously aware of being under an emotional overload.

**Focal neurological deficits:** Specific impairments in nerve function, such as weakness, sensory loss, or difficulties with vision or speech, which may occur as a result of mTBI.

**Gait disturbances:** Abnormalities in walking patterns, such as unsteadiness, shuffling, or difficulty maintaining balance, which can result from various neurological, musculoskeletal, or vestibular disorders affecting the coordination and control of movement.

**Head Injury (HI):** The term is applied to damage sustained by the brain, not the bony case (the cranium) which surrounds it.

**Headache:** Pain in the head or neck region.

**Healthcare services:** Medical care, treatments, and support provided by the VA to eligible veterans, including those with mTBI.

**Imaging tests:** Medical procedures that create visual representations of the brain, such as CT scans or MRI, which can help diagnose mTBI and identify structural damage.

**Immediate Post-Concussion Assessment and Cognitive Testing (ImPACT):** A computerized neurocognitive test that measures attention span, working memory, sustained and selective attention time, response variability, non-verbal problem solving, and reaction time.

**Impaired Learning:** Difficulty acquiring, processing, or retaining new information, which can be a cognitive symptom of mTBI.

**Impulsivity:** Impulsivity is acting without forethought, characterized by hasty decisions, lack of self-control, and a tendency to engage in risky or inappropriate behaviors.

**Insomnia:** Difficulty falling asleep or staying asleep.

**Intracranial hemorrhage:** Bleeding within the skull, either in the brain tissue, ventricles, or surrounding meninges, often caused by trauma or vascular malformations.

**Irritability:** Easily annoyed or angered.

**King-Devick (K-D) Test:** A rapid, simple measure of visual tracking, attention, and saccadic eye movements, involving reading aloud a series of single-digit numbers displayed in a specific pattern.

**Liver Failure:** A condition in which the liver loses its ability to function properly, which can be a severe adverse reaction to certain medications.

**Loss of consciousness:** A brief period of unresponsiveness following a head injury.

**Loss of memory:** Inability to remember events that occurred immediately before or after the traumatic event, known as anterograde or retrograde amnesia.

**Magnetic Resonance Imaging (MRI):** An imaging test that uses magnetic fields and radio waves to produce detailed brain images, helping to detect more subtle changes in brain tissue.

**Medication management:** The use of prescribed medications to help manage symptoms associated with mTBI, such as pain, headaches, or mood disturbances.

**Memory impairment:** Difficulty remembering new information or recalling past events.

**Migraine:** A severe, throbbing headache often accompanied by sensitivity to light and sound.

**Mild Traumatic Brain Injury (mTBI):** A type of brain injury resulting from a blow, jolt, or bump to the head that disrupts normal brain function.

**Mood changes:** Alterations in emotional state, such as irritability, anxiety, or depression.

**Motor coordination issues:** Motor coordination issues related to traumatic brain injury (TBI) involve difficulties with balance, fine motor skills, and smooth, coordinated movements due to damage to brain areas controlling motor function, leading to clumsiness, tremors, or difficulty with tasks requiring precise movements.

**Multidisciplinary teams:** Multidisciplinary teams that help traumatic brain injury (TBI) patients are composed of healthcare professionals from various specialties, including physicians, neuropsychologists, physical therapists, occupational therapists, speech-language pathologists, social workers, and rehabilitation nurses. These teams work collaboratively to assess, diagnose, and develop comprehensive treatment plans tailored to each patient's specific needs, goals, and stage of recovery. The team approach ensures coordinated care, addressing the physical, cognitive, emotional, and social aspects of TBI rehabilitation to optimize patient outcomes and quality of life.

**Nausea:** A feeling of sickness with an inclination to vomit.

**Neuroendocrine dysfunction:** Related to traumatic brain injury (TBI, a condition in which the hypothalamus, pituitary gland, or other parts of the neuroendocrine system are damaged, leading to imbalances in hormone production and regulation. This can result in various symptoms such as fatigue, mood changes, sexual dysfunction, sleep disturbances, temperature regulation issues, and abnormal growth. The severity and specific symptoms depend on the location and extent of the brain damage caused by the TBI.

**Neurological Examination:** An assessment of a patient's cognitive function, vision, hearing, balance, coordination, reflexes, and strength to identify any neurological impairments.

**Neurological examinations:** Assessments performed by healthcare providers to evaluate a person's nervous system function, including motor skills, sensory function, reflexes, and cognitive abilities.

**Neurodegenerative Diseases:** A group of disorders characterized by the progressive loss of structure or function of neurons, including diseases like Alzheimer's and Parkinson's, which have been linked to an increased risk following TBI.

**Oculomotor Assessments:** Tests that evaluate eye movements, tracking, and focus, which can be impaired following an mTBI, such as the King-Devick (K-D) Test and the Vestibular/Ocular Motor Screening (VOMS).

**Open Head Injury:** A traumatic brain injury in which the skull and dura mater are penetrated or compromised, exposing the brain to the external environment and increasing the risk of infection, tissue damage, and other complications.

**Personalized Rehabilitation:** An approach to rehabilitation that tailors treatment plans to an individual's specific needs, goals, and circumstances, taking into account the unique effects of their TBI.

**Phonophobia:** An extreme sensitivity to or fear of specific sounds, often leading to anxiety, distress, and avoidance of sound-related situations.

**Photophobia:** An abnormal sensitivity to light, causing discomfort or pain in the eyes.

**Polytrauma/TBI System of Care:** A specialized program established by the VA to provide comprehensive care and support for veterans with mTBI and other complex injuries.

**Post-concussive syndrome:** A complex disorder characterized by persistent symptoms following a concussion or mild traumatic brain injury. Symptoms may include headaches, dizziness, fatigue, irritability, insomnia, concentration difficulties, and memory problems. These symptoms can last for weeks, months, or even years after the initial injury.

**Post-Traumatic Amnesia (PTA):** The inability to remember continuous, day-to-day experiences or events that occur after the injury to the brain.

**Post-traumatic stress disorder (PTSD):** A mental health disorder that may develop after exposure to a traumatic event, characterized by symptoms such as intrusive memories, avoidance, negative changes in thinking and mood, and alterations in arousal and reactivity.

**Rehabilitation services:** Therapies and interventions designed to help veterans with mTBI regain or improve physical, cognitive, and functional abilities, such as physical therapy, occupational therapy, and speech-language therapy.

**Restlessness:** An inability to rest or relax.

**Retrograde amnesia:** The loss of memories formed before the onset of amnesia, often due to head trauma, surgery, infection, or severe psychological stress. The most recent memories are typically lost first, with more distant memories being better preserved.

**Retrograde or Pre-Traumatic Amnesia:** The loss of memories formed before a traumatic brain injury (TBI). It involves the inability to recall events, information, and personal experiences from a period preceding the TBI, with the duration varying depending on the severity of the injury.

**Seizures:** Related to traumatic brain injury (TBI), sudden, uncontrolled electrical disturbances in the brain that can cause changes in behavior, movements, feelings, and consciousness. They may occur immediately after the injury or develop later, and can be a single episode or recurrent. Severity and symptoms vary depending on the affected brain areas.

**Sensory Organization Test (SOT):** A sophisticated, computerized method of assessing balance that evaluates an individual's ability to maintain postural stability under various sensory conditions.

**Service-connected:** A term used to describe a disability or condition that was incurred or aggravated during active military service.

**Silent Epidemic:** A term used to describe the widespread occurrence of mTBIs that often go undiagnosed or unrecognized due to the lack of visible symptoms.

**Skull fracture:** A break in one or more bones of the skull.

**Sleep disturbances:** Changes in sleep patterns, such as sleeping more or less than usual.

**Slow processing speed:** Slow processing speed related to traumatic brain injury (TBI) is a cognitive impairment characterized by difficulties in quickly and efficiently processing information, resulting in longer times to understand, respond to, and complete tasks.

**Standardized Assessment of Concussion (SAC):** A brief, standardized screening tool that assesses cognitive function immediately following a suspected concussion, consisting of four components: orientation, immediate memory, concentration, and delayed recall.

**Strategy:** An operating plan designed to assist the individual in carrying out a task. A strategy may involve using one or more props.

**Stress:** A state of mental or emotional strain resulting from adverse or demanding circumstances, which can be exacerbated by mTBI.

**Tinnitus:** Related to traumatic brain injury (TBI), the perception of ringing, buzzing, or other sounds in one or both ears without an external source, often caused by damage to the auditory system resulting from the TBI.

**Traumatic Brain Injury (TBI):** A type of brain injury caused by a sudden, external force to the head, resulting in damage to the brain.

**Vertigo:** A sensation of spinning, swaying, or tilting, often accompanied by a feeling of disorientation, even when a person is stationary. It is not the same as dizziness or lightheadedness, which do not involve the perception of movement. People with vertigo may feel like they are moving or rotating, or that their surroundings are moving around them. Vertigo can be:
Subjective: The person feels like they are moving or spinning.
Objective: The person perceives that their surroundings are moving or spinning.
Vertigo is often caused by problems in the inner ear (vestibular system), which is responsible for maintaining balance and spatial orientation. Common causes of vertigo include:
a. Benign paroxysmal positional vertigo (BPPV): A condition where tiny crystals in the inner ear become dislodged and move into the fluid-filled canals, causing brief episodes of intense vertigo triggered by specific head movements.
b. Vestibular neuritis or labyrinthitis: Inflammation of the vestibular nerve or inner ear, often due to a viral infection, leading to sudden, severe vertigo lasting several days.

c. Meniere's disease: A disorder of the inner ear characterized by episodes of vertigo, fluctuating hearing loss, tinnitus (ringing in the ear), and a feeling of fullness in the ear.
d. Vestibular migraine: A type of migraine headache associated with vertigo and other vestibular symptoms.
e. Concussion or traumatic brain injury: Damage to the brain can disrupt the processing of sensory information, including signals from the vestibular system.
Other causes of vertigo may include stroke, multiple sclerosis, acoustic neuroma (a benign tumor of the vestibular nerve), or certain medications.
Symptoms of vertigo may last a few seconds to a few hours or more and can be triggered by specific movements, such as turning the head, looking up, or rolling over in bed. Vertigo can be debilitating and may cause nausea, vomiting, and difficulty walking or standing. Treatment depends on the underlying cause and may include vestibular rehabilitation therapy, medication (e.g., anti-nausea drugs, steroids), repositioning maneuvers (for BPPV), or surgery in rare cases.

**Vestibular/Balance Tests:** These tests assess a patient's ability to maintain balance and evaluate the function of the vestibular system, which is responsible for sensing head movement and providing information about balance and spatial orientation. Mild traumatic brain injury (mTBI) can disrupt vestibular function. Two common tests are:
a. Balance Error Scoring System (BESS): A simple, cost-effective test that assesses postural stability under different conditions, such as standing on a firm or foam surface with eyes closed. The number of errors (e.g., stepping out of position, opening eyes) is counted during each condition.
b. Sensory Organization Test (SOT): A more advanced test that uses a computerized platform to assess a patient's ability to maintain balance under different sensory conditions (e.g., eyes open/closed, stable/moving platform). It helps identify which

sensory systems (visual, vestibular, or somatosensory) the patient relies on most for balance.

**Vestibular/Ocular Motor Screening (VOMS):** VOMS is a comprehensive assessment tool designed to evaluate the function of the vestibular and ocular motor systems, which are often affected by mTBI. It consists of seven subtests that assess different aspects of these systems:
a. Smooth pursuit: The ability to follow a moving target smoothly with the eyes.
b. Saccades: The ability to quickly shift gaze between two targets.
c. Convergence: The ability to maintain focus on a target as it moves closer to the eyes.
d. Vestibular-ocular reflex: The ability to maintain stable vision during head movements.
e. Visual motion sensitivity: The ability to tolerate complex visual motion without experiencing dizziness or discomfort.
Each subtest is scored based on the presence and severity of symptoms (e.g., headache, dizziness, nausea) and the presence of objective signs (e.g., abnormal eye movements).

**Vision problems:** mTBI can cause various vision problems, such as:
a. Blurred vision: Difficulty seeing things clearly, as if looking through a fog or haze. b. Double vision (diplopia): Seeing two images of a single object, either side-by-side or one above the other.
c. Eye strain or fatigue: Eyes feeling tired or uncomfortable, especially after reading or using a computer.
d. Light sensitivity (photophobia): Discomfort or pain in the eyes when exposed to bright light.

**Vocational rehabilitation:** Vocational rehabilitation is a service provided by the Department of Veterans Affairs (VA) to help veterans with service-connected disabilities, including mTBI,

prepare for, find, and maintain suitable employment. It may include:
a. Vocational assessment: Evaluating a veteran's skills, interests, and abilities to identify appropriate career goals.
b. Training and education: Providing access to programs that help veterans acquire the skills and knowledge needed for their desired career.
c. Job search assistance: Helping veterans find job openings, create resumes, and prepare for interviews.
d. Workplace accommodations: Working with employers to ensure that veterans have the necessary accommodations to perform their job duties effectively.
The goal of vocational rehabilitation is to help veterans with disabilities, such as mTBI, overcome barriers to employment and achieve their career goals.

**Vomiting**: The forceful expulsion of stomach contents through the mouth. It is a reflex action controlled by the brain, specifically the vomiting center in the medulla oblongata. Vomiting occurs when the stomach muscles and diaphragm contract simultaneously, pushing the stomach contents up through the esophagus and out of the mouth. Common causes of vomiting include:
a. Gastroenteritis (stomach flu)
b. Food poisoning
c. Motion sickness
d. Migraine headaches
e. Concussion or traumatic brain injury
f. Chemotherapy or radiation therapy
g. Pregnancy (morning sickness)
Vomiting can lead to dehydration and electrolyte imbalances, so it is important to replace lost fluids and seek medical attention if vomiting persists or is accompanied by other symptoms such as fever, severe abdominal pain, or blood in the vomit.

**Whiplash**: A neck injury caused by sudden, forceful back-and-forth movement of the head, resembling the cracking of a whip. It is most commonly associated with rear-end car accidents but can also occur during sports activities, physical abuse, or other traumatic events. The rapid movement can stretch and tear the muscles, tendons, and ligaments in the neck, leading to symptoms such as:

a. Neck pain and stiffness
b. Headaches, especially at the base of the skull
c. Dizziness
d. Blurred vision
e. Fatigue
f. Shoulder, arm, or back pain
g. Numbness or tingling in the arms.
h. Difficulty concentrating or memory problems.
i. Sleep disturbances
j. Irritability or mood changes

Symptoms of whiplash may appear immediately after the injury or develop days or weeks later. Treatment typically involves pain management (e.g., over-the-counter pain relievers, ice/heat therapy), physical therapy to improve neck range of motion and strength, and in some cases, a cervical collar to provide support and limit neck movement. Most people recover from whiplash within a few weeks to a few months, but some may experience chronic pain or other long-term complications.

# ABOUT THE AUTHOR

Michael Hackard, Esq., is the founder of Hackard Law, a California law firm focused on several areas of law, including representing victims of traumatic brain injury (TBI). He practiced law for over 45 years before writing It's Never Just an Accident and has been interviewed repularly by local and national media, including The Wall Street Journal, C-SPAN and Fox News, and has testified before the U.S. House of Representatives.

# ALSO BY MICHAEL HACKARD, ESQ.

Michael has also written the books *The Wolf at the Door: Undue Influence and Elder Financial Abuse* and *Alzheimer's, Widowed Stepmothers & Estate Crimes: Cause, Action, and Response in Cases of Fractured Inheritance, Lost Inheritance, and Disinheritance*.

www.ingramcontent.com/pod-product-compliance
Lightning Source LLC
Chambersburg PA
CBHW031153020426
42333CB00013B/650